DEMONS

THE ANSWER BOOK

DEMONS

THE ANSWER BOOK

LESTER SUMRALL

WHITAKER
HOUSE

Unless otherwise indicated, all Scripture quotations are taken from the King James Version (KJV) of the Holy Bible. Scripture quotations marked (RSV) are from the *Revised Standard Version Common Bible* © 1973, by the Division of Christian Education of the National Council of Churches of Christ in the U.S.A. Used by permission.

DEMONS: THE ANSWER BOOK
updated edition

ISBN: 978-0-88368-955-4
eBook ISBN: 978-1-60374-800-1
Printed in the United States of America
© 1979, 2003 by Lester Sumrall Evangelistic Association, Inc.

Whitaker House
1030 Hunt Valley Circle
New Kensington, PA 15068
www.whitakerhouse.com

Library of Congress Cataloging-in-Publication Data
Sumrall, Lester Frank, 1913–
Demons : the answer book / Lester Sumrall.—Updated ed.
p. cm.
ISBN 0-88368-955-3 (pbk.)
1. Demonology. I. Title.
BT975.S93 2003
235'.4—dc22
2003017379

12 13 14 15 16 **WH** 26 25 24 23

Contents

Introduction

I t is a pity that in a great country like ours, with its freedom of the press and millions of Bibles, books, and magazines, people know less about demon power than citizens of Africa or Tibet do. Possibly through gross neglect, the ministers of our generation have not informed the people of the reality of demon power.

There are three sources of power common to human understanding. (1) *Divine power,* or power that proceeds from the omnipotence of God; (2) *satanic power,* or power coming from Lucifer the fallen archangel (see Isaiah 14); and (3) *human power,* or the power of man. This third power is a neutral force that can be directed by heavenly or demonic powers.

God has given man the authority and right to choose his lifestyle and destiny. He created man to rule and have dominion over all creation. (See Genesis 1:26–27.)

The devil wishes to enslave man and steal his dominion. Quite the opposite, Jesus wants mankind to be free. In Luke 13:16, Jesus said that a woman whom the devil had bound should be loosed. Christ sent His disciples to loose the human race.

The purpose of this book is to reveal the actual powers operating in our world and our lives.

— Lester Sumrall

I
Bitten by Demons

Master, I have brought unto thee my son,
which hath a dumb spirit; and wheresoever
he taketh him, he teareth him.

—Mark 9:17–18

On May 12, 1953, the *Daily Mirror* in Manila carried a highly unusual story under the headline "Police Medic Explodes Biting Demons Yarn."

A city jail inmate puzzled police and medical examiners with her tale about two devils biting her....Sergeant Guillermo Abad, detailed with the city jail last night, said the girl claimed she was bitten twenty times, and she shouted every time she was hurt.

In the jail last night she talked and answered questions weakly, but sensibly, before a crowd of observers. Suddenly her facial expressions

9

would change to anguish and horror as if she were confronted with "The Thing." She would look around wildly and then scream and struggle and hit her arms and shoulders....Then her strenuous resistance would cease and she would collapse into the arms of those holding her, weak and half-conscious.

After regaining her senses, she said that one of the devils was big and dark with curly hair on his head, chest, and arms. He had large, sharp eyes and two fangs. His voice was a deep, echoing sound. He was shrouded in black....

She was bitten for the last time on the right knee. That was the first bite on the lower part of her anatomy. Other bite marks appear on her neck, arms, and shoulders. Observers insist that they are within sight the entire time.

The following day the *Manila Chronicle* reported further news of the young woman, Clarita Villanueva:

At least twenty-five competent persons, including Manila's chief of police, Col. Cesar Lucero, say that it is a very realistic example of a horrified woman being bitten to insanity by "invisible persons." She displayed several bite marks all over her body, inflicted by nobody as far as the twenty-five witnesses could see. Villanueva writhed in pain, shouted and screamed in anguish whenever the "invisible demons" attacked her.

Fr. Benito Vargas (Roman Catholic)...who witnessed Villanueva in her fits said it was not his to conclude any verdict. But he said the fact remains that "I saw her bitten three times."

Villanueva was perfectly normal between fits. After talking for a while, she would shout, have convulsions and hysterics, all the time screaming, and her eyes flashing with fire. Then she would point to a part of her body being attacked, then fall almost senseless into the hands of investigators. Teeth marks, wet with saliva, marked the spots she pointed at.

At the time, I was founding a church in Manila. The newspaper accounts had not caught my attention, but a forty-five-minute radio program over station DZFM drew me into it personally. The radio announcer dramatically opened the broadcast: "Good evening, ladies and gentlemen. If you have a weak heart, please turn your radio off!"

I turned the volume of our radio higher. Instantly, I heard piercing screams followed by pandemonium. Doctors spoke out of the confusion: "This can all be explained!...Our records show that this phenomenon has been known before....This is epilepsy....It is extreme hysteria."

Others were excitedly saying, "Look, the marks of teeth appear!" Another said, "The girl is being choked by some unseen thing. She is blue in the face and there are marks on her neck." Then Clarita would scream again.

Listening to this in the comfort of our bedroom, I turned to my wife and said, "The girl is not sick, and the doctors are helpless before such an enemy. Her cry is the cry of the damned and doomed; that girl is demon-possessed."

It was impossible for me to sleep after listening to the program. I walked the floor, crying to God to deliver the poor girl in the city jail. But the longer I prayed, the heavier the load became upon my soul. I said, "Oh God, if the devil is in that girl, You can cast him out! Please do it!"

After praying until morning, God spoke to my heart: "If you will go to the jail and pray for her, I will deliver her."

But I didn't want to go. I found myself answering, "No, God. I can never go to that place. Scientists, professors, legal experts, and even spiritualists have been trying to help that girl. They all have had adverse publicity in the newspapers. I cannot go."

The Lord replied, "If you will go and pray for her, I will deliver her."

"No," was my reply.

But I found I could no longer pray for her. When I cried for her deliverance, my conscience stopped me, saying, "You are not sincere, for you refuse to go and see her." Finally I decided to go to Bilibid prison and pray for the girl.

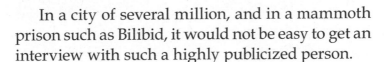

In a city of several million, and in a mammoth prison such as Bilibid, it would not be easy to get an interview with such a highly publicized person.

On my way to town the following morning I stopped at the home of the architect who had designed our church, Leopoldo Coronel, a personal friend of the Manila mayor. At my request, we visited Mayor Lacson and gained permission for me to pray for Clarita, but on one condition. Dr. Mariano Lara, chief medical adviser of the police department, must also grant permission. Mr. Coronel did not know Dr. Lara, but an interview was arranged through another friend.

Mr. Coronel and I arrived at Bilibid prison and were escorted to the morgue to see Dr. Lara. The surroundings were eerie. The first thing I noticed was a cadaver on the table. Another corpse lay wrapped in a blanket on a stretcher, awaiting attention. On a table were a dozen or more jars of alcohol containing parts of human beings. We found out later that these were for student demonstrations.

Sitting on a bench in this drab place, Dr. Lara told us about himself. He was a professor and the head of pathology and legal medicine at the Manila Central University and professorial lecturer of legal medicine at the University of Santo Tomas. In his thirty-eight years of medical practice he had performed more than eight thousand autopsies, and he had never accepted the theory of a nonmaterial force existing in the universe.

Dr. Lara had not intended to be drawn into the Clarita Villanueva affair. On May 12, upon entering the office of one of his medical assistants, he first observed the young prisoner. Noticing the reddish, human-like bite impressions on her arms, both physicians believed Clarita had bitten herself. Considering her "abnormal," they agreed to recommend her for treatment in the national psychopathic hospital.

The following day, however, at the insistence of visitors who wanted to know Dr. Lara's medical opinion, he had her brought to the medical examiner's office in the police department. A class of interns was also there. According to the doctor, Clarita was unconscious when she was carried to the room. This is what he told me:

> Her arms lifted by me would fall without resistance. Pointed needles and pins touching her skin gave no response throughout her body surface. After several minutes in this condition, Clarita began to come out of this state of insensibility and trance.
>
> Meanwhile, I was like Sherlock Holmes of the detective stories, or Dr. Cyclops, the film character. Equipped with a magnifying lens and an unbelieving mind about this biting phenomenon, I scrutinized carefully the exposed parts of her body—her arms, hands, and neck—to find out whether they had the biting impressions....She was still weak in her entire body and could not stand up by

herself. One of my assistants, a cadaver tech-
nician, Alfonso by name, helped carry her to
a bed for her to rest during this state of par-
tial trance. Alfonso got hold of her body and
deposited her on the prepared bed, placing
both her hands over her in order that they
would not hang downward.

At that very instant, this girl in a semi-
trance loudly screamed repeatedly the word
"aruy" [a scream of pain in Tagalog], and
when I removed Alfonso's hand from Clarita's I saw with my unbelieving eyes the clear
marks or impressions of human-like teeth
from both the upper and lower jaws. It was
a little moist in the area bitten on the dorsal
aspect of the left hand, and the teeth impressions were mostly from the form of the front
or incisor teeth....

I could not understand or explain how the
bites were produced, as her hand had all the
time been held away from the reach of her
mouth. The place where the bite impressions
occurred, on the dorsal of the left hand, was
the very place held by my assistant Alfonso.
I knew she could not bite herself nor could
Alfonso, who does not possess a single tooth,
having recently had them extracted. And I am
sure I did not bite the girl! Not finding any
possible explanation insofar as my human
experience in medical training was concerned,
I kept my mouth shut, but not my mind.

Clarita kept on screaming for about fif-
teen minutes with this bite on her left hand,

and she turned bluish in the face and legs as if being choked. There were also a few reddish whelps in the front of the neck....After about twenty minutes of this attack, accompanied by stiffness and screaming, her body became soft and in a trance-like condition—a repetition of the observation made when she was first brought into the room. After about ten minutes of this trance and softness of the entire body, she gradually recovered consciousness and, shortly thereafter, became normal again.

In this normal condition she sat on a chair, and the group of interns talked with her. She answered all the questions they asked her sanely and intelligently, and she told us the following: She was born in Bacolod City in the province of Negros Occidental. She has several brothers but is not interested in them as they have been unkind to her. Her parents died several years ago.

I asked her who was causing her to suffer from the bites. She answered that there were two who were alternately biting her; one big, black, hairy human-like fellow, very tall and with two sharp eyes, two sharp canine teeth, a long beard like a Hindu, hairy extremities and chest, wearing a black garment with a little whitish piece on the back resembling a hood. His feet were about three times the size of normal feet. The other fellow was a very small one, about two or three feet tall, allegedly also black, hairy, and ugly.

This baffling Filipino girl had changed Dr. Lara's philosophy of life. He turned to me and said, "Reverend, I am humble enough to admit that I am a frightened man."

I realized that my first objective was to convince Dr. Lara that I knew what I was doing and that I knew how to help this girl. I began slowly.

"There are only three powers in the universe," I said. "There is the 'positive power,' or the power of a creative and benevolent God. There is the 'human power,' or the power of men here on the earth. And there is the 'negative power,' or the malevolent and sinister power of the devil. These powers are real and evident around us. Now, do you think Clarita is acting under God's power?"

He shook his head slowly and replied, "No, not God's power."

"Then do you feel that, with your experience with human beings, she is acting like any human being?"

"No, the actions of this girl are not related to human beings," he said.

"Then there is only one power left," I told him. "She must be acting under demon power."

Dr. Lara explained that his broad experiences as a medical man had not prepared him for an encounter with something that was beyond doubt "supernatural."

I continued, "Dr. Lara, if there is a negative force in the universe over which a positive force has no control, our universe would go to pieces. If there is an evil that no right can correct, then evil is mightier than right. This cannot be. If this girl has demon power working in her, then Jesus Christ can deliver her from that power."

I turned to the gospel of Mark and read, "*'And these signs shall follow them that believe; In my name shall they cast out devils'* (Mark 16:17). Do you believe this?" I asked.

Dr. Lara looked at me and said, "I believe, but who will help us?" He thought spiritual assistance was out of the question. The Roman Catholic chaplain of Bilibid prison, the Catholic archbishop of the Philippines, and priests of the Roman Catholic healing center at Baclaran had all refused to pray for her.

I told him I would be glad to go and pray for the girl if he would permit it. He said I would be welcome. I requested that no medication be given to her during the time I would be praying for her and that no other groups be permitted to pray for her or offer assistance in any way. If Jesus healed her, He must have all the glory. He agreed, and an appointment was made for me to return the following morning. I fasted the rest of the day, spending the time in prayer and reading the Word of God.

Upon entering the dreary walls of Bilibid prison the following morning, I felt there was going to be a contest between the God of Elijah and the prophets of Baal. Ancient Bilibid, with its centuries of bloody history, was to witness a new kind of battle. Here the Spaniards had imprisoned their victims. Here the Japanese had conducted uncounted atrocities. Here American missionaries had almost starved until the day of liberation. And now there were hundreds of lawbreakers behind its stockades. It was an uninviting place to pray the prayer of deliverance.

On this first morning, Leopoldo Coronel accompanied me. We met Dr. Lara and a professor from the Far Eastern University and started walking toward the women's cellblock. Upon seeing the police officers, newspapermen, and photographers who were gathered, I could almost hear the devil whispering, "Just as I told you! Now you have made a fool of yourself!"

Following behind us was a motley crowd without the slightest idea of what they were going to see. By the time we had assembled in a small chapel for women prisoners, there must have been a hundred spectators, including prisoners.

At first I felt that my greatest battle would be with the spectators, but they were friendly and even sympathetic. Most of them had already seen the teeth bites on the girl. They had observed the failure of the doctors and psychiatrists and spiritualists. But they had never heard prayer for the diseased and demon-possessed.

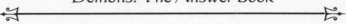

Steel bars covered the windows of the small chapel. A primitive Catholic altar stood at one end of the dreary room. The only other furnishings were a wooden bunk and a couple of small hand-made chairs.

After we all gathered in the chapel, Dr. Lara asked that Clarita be brought in. She observed each person slowly and closely as she entered the room. When she came to me at the end of the line, her eyes widened, and she glared at me, saying, "I don't like you!"

These were the first words the devil spoke through her lips to me. The demons used her lips constantly to curse me, to curse God, and to curse the blood of Christ. She did this in English, yet after she was delivered I had to converse with her through an interpreter, as she could not speak English.

I had her sit on a wooden bench, and I drew up a chair in front of her.

"Clarita," I said, "I have come to deliver you from the power of these devils in the name of Jesus Christ, the Son of God."

Suddenly she went into a fit of rage, screaming, "No, no! They will kill me!" Her body became rigid, and she lost consciousness. This had baffled the doctors when they had tried to analyze her case, but I had dealt with devils before and understood some of their antics. Taking hold of her head with both hands I cried, "'Come out of her, you evil and wicked spirit of hell. Come out of her in Jesus' name!"

Immediately she began to rage again. This was the first time she had instantly come back from one of the trances. With tears flowing down her cheeks she begged me to leave her alone; she showed me terrible marks on her arms and neck where she had been bitten that moment. I was shocked. The teeth marks were so severe that some of the small blood vessels beneath the skin were broken. Rather than feeling like quitting, I simply forgot that I was surrounded with unbelievers and went into the greatest battle of my life.

The devils would curse God, and I would demand them to quit and tell them God is holy. Then they would curse the blood of Jesus and I rebuked them, reminding them that He is the Master over every evil power and that His blood is holy. Then they cursed me in the vilest language. They declared they would never leave. It seemed that the powers of darkness and the powers of righteousness were in deadly conflict. I was the mouthpiece for righteousness. Clarita was the mouthpiece of the devil. Undoubtedly the noise could be heard for some distance in the prison.

Finally it seemed that the girl was relieved. The devils refused to talk to me or to bite her. Some of those present thought she was delivered, but I told them she was not. It was nearly noon, and I was

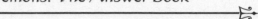
soaked with perspiration and nearly exhausted. When I looked around, I saw several of the people with tears in their eyes, moved by the things they had seen.

I told Dr. Lara that I desired to go home and fast and pray for another day, and then return the following morning. That day was spent in communion with God. It was precious. I could feel God's presence hovering over me, urging me not to be afraid.

However, I felt almost defeated because the evening newspapers had my picture on the front page, three columns wide, and a headline saying, "'The Thing' Defies Pastor." But God kept urging me to return.

That night, Rev. Arthur Ahlberg and Rev. Robert McAlister visited me at home and offered to go with me the following day. They would stand between me and the crowd and keep them from getting too close during prayer.

Upon our arrival at Bilibid the following morning, the captain of the prison said Clarita had not been bitten since the prayer. But I knew she was not yet delivered. This became evident as soon as the devils saw me. Through her lips they cried, "Go away! Go away!"

I sat on the same small chair in front of her and spoke back with a thrilling feeling of authority. "No, I am not going away, but you are going away! This girl will be delivered today!"

Then I requested every person present to kneel—
there were as many present as the day before, or
more. Doctors, newspapermen, police officers, and
professors humbly knelt as I prayed.

The battle began again. The devils realized it
was their last struggle. They cursed and held on
to their victim, begging permission to stay in her.
Then they cursed her for not responding, but it was
different on this day. The additional time of fasting
and prayer had made a difference.

Finally I felt the release and knew they had
departed. Clarita relaxed. The demon look departed
from her eyes. She smiled.

I looked around and noticed that reporters were
weeping; there were tears in the eyes of doctors;
hard-boiled jailers were also weeping. I could now
see how terrific the battle had been.

Softly I began to sing with brothers Ahlberg
and McAlister:

Oh, the blood of Jesus
Oh, the blood of Jesus
Oh, the blood of Jesus
That washes white as snow! [1]

On the second time around, the Filipinos joined in.
The atmosphere seemed clean inside that prison.

I asked Clarita if the devils were gone and she
answered in her own language, "Yes."

"Where did they go?"

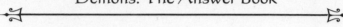
"Out that window," she replied.

We were ready to leave when suddenly, like a flash of lightning, the devils reappeared. The girl screamed and her eyes changed.

I said to them, "Why have you returned? You know you must go and not return."

Speaking in English through her lips they replied, "But she is unclean. We have a right to live in her."

I answered them in a determined voice. "Mary Magdalene was unclean with seven like you, but Jesus came into her life and she became clean by His mighty power. Therefore, I command you now to depart, and Jesus will make her clean."

They had no power to resist. They left, and she became normal again. I explained to her what had happened and got her to pray with me for the forgiveness of her sins.

As we were preparing to leave, the same thing was repeated. The unconverted newspapermen could not understand what was happening. Again I questioned the demons why they had returned and they said, "She has not asked us to go. She wants us. It is only you who desires for us to leave."

Again I demanded that they leave her and again they left immediately. I explained to her why they had returned and demanded her to tell them to leave and not return. This she did. Then I taught her to pray and plead the blood of Jesus against them.

It was now about noon, and Clarita was weak from the ordeal. I told the prison officers to give her rest and, after that, food.

As I was leaving I told Clarita that I was sure these devils would return. "After I am gone," I said, "they will come. Then you must demand them to leave without my being present. You must say, 'Go, in Jesus' name,' and they will obey." With this I left the compound.

We asked the newsmen not to write about the morning's events, but they said they were obligated to. The story had run for two weeks and it must be concluded. Since the Methodist church is the oldest Protestant denomination in the islands, they presumed I was a Methodist, and it was in the papers that way. They did not know how to write of such an experience; therefore, some of what they said was not correct. But I feel mostly responsible for this, as I gave them no interview and left the city to get away from publicity.

The devils did return to attack Clarita, and a strange thing happened when she called on them to leave. She was engaged in a mortal struggle and went into a coma, her fists clenched. The doctor pried her hands open and to his astonishment, there lay some long, black, coarse hair. Dr. Lara placed this hair in an envelope and put it in a guarded place. Under the microscope, he found that the hair was not from any part of the human body. The doctor has no answer to this mystery—how an invisible being, presumably a devil, could have lost hair by a visible being pulling it out. This phenomenon we must leave unanswered at the present.

On May 28, a headline in the *Manila Chronicle* read: "Victim of 'The Thing' Says Torturer Has Disappeared."

"The Thing" is dead! This every believer can now proclaim as Clarita Villanueva... claimed yesterday that "The Thing" has finally been exorcised.

Clarita told of her deliverance from her attackers as she pleaded for mercy before Judge Natividad Almeda-Lopez, who was to have tried her on vagrancy and prostitution charges.

The girl said the prayers of an American minister, Dr. Lester F. Sumrall, who purposely visited her to purge the devil, did it. Since Friday, May 22, when the minister prayed with her at the city jail chapel for women, "The Thing" had never appeared again, Clarita added.

Judge Almeda-Lopez placed Clarita in Welfareville, an institution for wayward girls, for observation. With Dr. Lara, I went to visit her twice and found her overjoyed at our coming. She rushed to us, saying she had feared she would never see us again. She hurried to bring us chairs and sat and talked with us at length. She did not seem like the same girl we had known in Bilibid prison, tormented by devils, her face distorted, screaming at the top of her voice. This was a perfectly normal Filipino girl who had recovered from the nightmare of demon possession.

Let the enemies of the Cross say what they will; Christ had conquered, and she who was bound was now set free!

Clarita was soon granted parole and placed in the home of a Christian family. After a time, in order to escape the curious people who wished to see her, she went to the north of Luzon and settled in a small town there.

It is not easy to give a detailed report of such a sensational story as this. In my travels in more than one hundred countries and more than one thousand cities of the world, I have not heard anything so amazing. The following facts are indisputable and unassailable: Clarita was bitten and choked by unseen adversaries. Her case could not be solved by medical or psychological science. She was delivered by the power of simple prayer to Christ. The glory and praise for this miracle we unreservedly give to God and the Lord Jesus Christ.

Notes

1. Source unknown.

2

Who Is the Devil and What Are Demons?

For still our ancient Foe
Doth seek to work us woe;
His craft and pow'r are great,
And, armed with cruel hate,
On earth is not his equal.

—Martin Luther,
"A Mighty Fortress Is Our God"

I feel very strongly that the devil is making his last attempt to capture the planet Earth. Reading about the final days of Howard Hughes, I was distressed to see how he died like an animal. He was so fearful that he wore gloves all the time so he would not contract disease. His private automobile was equipped with a

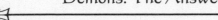

germproof, air-filtering system that cost $15,000. He recycled the well water on his private golf course to be sure he would not be contaminated by germs when he played golf. All his money could not free him from his fears.

There are those in Hollywood, I am told, whose lives are so full of fear and torment that they live completely abnormal lives. Their predicament is caused by the devil. Fear is fostered by an evil spirit.

The late Pope Paul VI said, "Whole societies have fallen under the domination of the devil. Sex and narcotics provide openings for Satan's infiltration of mankind. One of the great needs of our time is a defense against that evil which we call the devil. We all are under an obscure domination. It is by Satan, the Prince of this World, the number one enemy."

It was only a few years ago that those who took a stand against demons were criticized. They were not believed. Now that time is gone. Christians want information on how to discern demon power. They want to know how to exorcise demons and how to keep people free from satanic forces.

The devil's best defense has been his successful delusion of mankind into thinking he does not really exist. If we swallow that lie, we are simply proving how clever he is and how unbelievably naive we humans can be.

The Scriptures Are the Source of Information

In the Bible, Satan is directly mentioned more than two hundred times. Satan enters the realm of human activity in Genesis 3. In Job 1, he is an oppressor of good people. In Matthew 4, Satan audaciously tempts Jesus. His final incarceration and eternal confinement are described in Revelation 20.

We have the full story of the fall, the works, and the destiny of the devil in Ezekiel 28:

Son of man, take up a lamentation upon the king of Tyrus, and say unto him, Thus saith the Lord GOD; Thou sealest up the sum, full of wisdom, and perfect in beauty. Thou hast been in Eden the garden of God; every precious stone was thy covering, the sardius, topaz, and the diamond, the beryl, the onyx, and the jasper, the sapphire, the emerald, and the carbuncle, and gold: the workmanship of thy tabrets and of thy pipes was prepared in thee in the day that thou wast created. Thou art the anointed cherub that covereth; and I have set thee so: thou wast upon the holy mountain of God; thou hast walked up and down in the midst of the stones of fire. Thou wast perfect in thy ways from the day that thou wast created, till iniquity was found in thee. By the multitude of thy merchandise they have filled the midst of thee with violence, and thou hast sinned: therefore I will cast thee as profane out of the mountain of God: and I will destroy thee,

*O covering cherub, from the midst of the stones
of fire. Thine heart was lifted up because of thy
beauty, thou hast corrupted thy wisdom by reason
of thy brightness: I will cast thee to the ground,
I will lay thee before kings, that they may behold
thee. Thou hast defiled thy sanctuaries by the multitude of thine iniquities, by the iniquity of thy traf-
fic; therefore will I bring forth a fire from the midst
of thee, it shall devour thee, and I will bring thee
to ashes upon the earth in the sight of all them that
behold thee. All they that know thee among the
people shall be astonished at thee: thou shalt be a
terror, and never shalt thou be any more.*

(Ezek. 28:12–19)

Satan was created an archangel, one of the
highest order of God's creation. This description in
Ezekiel can only be applied to a super-being, not a
man who ruled Tyre.

The prophet Isaiah described the devil's actual
fall from his place of honor and glory as one of the
archangels.

*How art thou fallen from heaven, O Lucifer, son of
the morning! how art thou cut down to the ground,
which didst weaken the nations! For thou hast said
in thine heart, I will ascend into heaven, I will exalt
my throne above the stars of God: I will sit also upon
the mount of the congregation, in the sides of the
north: I will ascend above the heights of the clouds;
I will be like the most High.* (Isa. 14:12–14)

The apostle John supplied more description of
Satan's fall:

And there was war in heaven: Michael and his angels fought against the dragon; and the dragon fought and his angels, and prevailed not; neither was their place found any more in heaven. And the great dragon was cast out, that old serpent, called the Devil, and Satan, which deceiveth the whole world: he was cast out into the earth, and his angels were cast out with him. And I heard a loud voice saying in heaven, Now is come salvation, and strength, and the kingdom of our God, and the power of his Christ: for the accuser of our brethren is cast down, which accused them before our God day and night....Therefore rejoice, ye heavens, and ye that dwell in them. Woe to the inhabiters of the earth and of the sea! for the devil is come down unto you, having great wrath, because he knoweth that he hath but a short time. (Rev. 12:7–10, 12)

Not content to be the beautiful, intelligent creature of God's creation and the highest order of angels, Satan aspired to a position of equality with God. His contest seems to have been most specifically with Jesus Christ, although the entire Godhead was challenged. This conflict has endured through the ages and will not be entirely resolved until Satan is cast into the lake of fire forever.

Satan's Power

The devil's titles, abilities, and sphere of influence are clearly defined. In the tabernacle and temple in Jerusalem in Ezekiel 28:14, he is called *"the anointed cherub that covereth."* The cherubim were in the most holy place of worship during Old Testament days. Two golden-winged cherubim formed a part of the mercy seat or covering of the holy ark of the covenant, which was the symbol of Israel's holiest devotion to Jehovah. The anointed cherub had to do with the very holiness of God.

Satan Was Beautiful

He was perhaps the most gorgeous creature of all. His form was covered with gold and the most costly of stones. Ezekiel wrote that he was *"perfect in beauty"* (v. 12).

Melody and Music

Satan was evidently the first created being. The description in Ezekiel 28:13 includes a reference to musical instruments—"tabrets and pipes"—indicating that he had the ability to create lovely music. Some believe that, before his fall, he led musical praise to God. Certainly the devil makes tremendous use of music today.

From an Angel to a Devil

Satan fell first because of pride over his personal beauty. (See Ezekiel 28:17.) His greed and lust for physical and material things supplanted his spiritual service to Jehovah. He is spoken of in verse 18 as having a "multitude of iniquities" that led him to be full of violence. Perhaps this is a reference to his seeking after all things with no regard for whom he hurt in the quest.

These elements—pride and greed—have been major tools in tempting man to sin ever since. How many of us commit sin out of pride of possession and pride of physical beauty? If these could produce iniquity in the *"cherub that covereth,"* how easily will they produce iniquity in sinful flesh like ours!

Satan Is Still a Dignitary

In the book of Jude, we read that the archangel Michael, an angel of great power and position in heaven, *"did not presume to pronounce a reviling judgment upon him* [Satan]" (v. 9, RSV) when disputing over Moses' body. Even in his fallen state, the devil is one of the most intelligent and keenest personalities created by God.

Lucifer, the Devil, Is a Real Person

The devil is not an influence or an idea or some abstract design. He is a person. Personal names and titles are given to him (Rev. 20:2). Personal acts and attributes are ascribed to him (Isa. 14:12–15). Jesus dealt with the devil as a person (Matt. 4:1–11) and waged war against him as against a person (Luke 13:16). Paul, in his epistles, described the believer's battle with Satan as with a real person (Eph. 6:10–18). The devil is spoken of as possessing personal characteristics—heart, pride, speech, knowledge, power, desire, and lusts. (For a complete list of the names of the devil as used in Scripture, see Appendix.)

What Are Demons?

In several places Scripture speaks of angels that are aligned with the devil. In the famous passage about the kingdom of heaven, in Matthew 25:31–46, Jesus spoke of the *"everlasting fire, prepared for the devil and his angels"* (v. 41).

The most explicit description is in the book of Revelation. John was shown a vision of a *"wonder in heaven...a great red dragon"* (Rev. 12:3) in which the archangel Michael and his angels wage battle against this serpent.

> *And the great dragon was cast out, that old serpent, called the Devil, and Satan, which deceiveth the whole world: he was cast out into the earth, and his angels were cast out with him.* (v. 9)

This same passage speaks of the dragon sweeping a third of the stars of heaven down with his tail (v. 4). Many commentators interpret stars as angels—that Satan caused a third of the heavenly hosts to rebel with him when he arrogantly tried to be like God. Since the angels are without number, *"ten thousand times ten thousand, and thousands of thousands"* (Rev. 5:11), the sheer number of Satan's angels is beyond our mind's grasp.

These angels are the demons—or evil, unclean spirits—the Bible speaks of. Their name comes from the Latin word *daemon,* meaning "evil spirit," and from the Greek word *daimon,* meaning "a divinity."

Demons Are Ageless

From the Bible we understand that large numbers of demons roam the earth and the air. Since they do not die, they have been in the world since the beginning of time.

Demons Are Personalities

These demons are personalities without bodies, and they are highly organized. As fallen spirits they desire to dwell in a body in order to manifest themselves. They are angry with God because of their fallen state; their prime motive is to destroy what God loves or creates—chiefly, man.

In our travels we have heard of demon spirits who claimed to have been Napoleon, Alexander the Great, and other world leaders. They often state the names of people they have lived in previously. When someone who is possessed of a devil dies, that spirit immediately seeks a dwelling place in another person. He cannot walk into just any person's life; he must find one with an open door. If he is a spirit of lust, he seeks a lustful person. If he is a spirit of anger, he seeks to possess a person who has little control over his temper. A spirit of insanity will seek to enter a person's troubled mind.

Paul Warned of Demon Power

That demons are highly organized can be seen from the concluding passage of the apostle Paul's letter to the Ephesians:

> For we wrestle not against flesh and blood, but against principalities, against powers, against the rulers of the darkness of this world, against spiritual wickedness in high places.   (Eph. 6:12)

Satan and his demon-angels have their abode and base of operation in the high places.

Jesus Cast Out Demons

Jesus took for granted the existence of demons. He dealt with them constantly, casting them out of the people (Matt. 15:22, 28) and giving His disciples the power to set people free (Matt. 10:1; Luke 9:1; Mark 16:17).

The Apostles Believed in the Existence of Demons

The apostles believed firmly in the existence of demons. Matthew suggested their organization under Satan (Matt. 12:26) and spoke of their final doom (Matt. 25:41). Luke described their nature (Luke 4:33; 6:18), their expulsion from human beings (Luke 9:42), and their place of dwelling (Luke 8:27–33).

John also told of their dwelling place (Rev. 9:11), their activity (Rev. 16:14), and declared their existence

(Rev. 9:20). Paul wrote to Timothy, warning him of *"doctrines of devils"* (1 Tim. 4:1).

Demons Name Themselves

Very often demons name themselves. The Bible denotes several examples. The spirits in the demon-possessed man of Gadara called themselves *"Legion"* (Mark 5:9). A demon once told me he was "serpent spirit," and another said loudly, "I am the angel over blood."

Demons Are Liars

We must realize, however, that demons are liars and may not be telling the truth about their names, numbers, or strength. Evidently they vary in wickedness; some can be *"more wicked"* than others (Matt. 12:45).

Demons Vary in Power

They also vary in power (Mark 9:29) and they seem to know the names of those who rebuke them and exorcise them. In Acts 19:15 an evil spirit said, *"Jesus I know, and Paul I know; but who are ye?"*

Demons Believe and Tremble

Demons are not dead people any more than angels are glorified believers who have died and gone to heaven. Demons believe in God, and as James said, they *"tremble"* (James 2:19). Their belief

is not one of faith and trust and commitment; rather, it is rather one of knowledge.

Demons Have Willpower

Demons have willpower (Matt. 12:44); they oppose saints and have doctrines (Rom. 8:38–39, 1 Tim. 4:1); and they do not abide in the truth (John 8:44). But the chief thing we all need to remember is that they are subject to—they are under—the sovereignty of the Lord Jesus Christ. Peter reminded his first-century fellow believers of that when he wrote of Jesus: *"Who is gone into heaven, and is on the right hand of God; angels and authorities and powers being made subject unto him"* (1 Pet. 3:22).

3
How Jesus Dealt
with the Devil

+✦————————✦+

The devil is afraid of persisting,
because he shrinks from frequent defeat.

—Ambrose

Jesus said more about devils than He did about
angels. He had more to say about hell than
heaven. On reading portions of the Gospels,
one quickly sees that much of Jesus' time was taken
up with encounters with evil spirits. They seemed
to crop up everywhere. In the opening chapter of
Mark's gospel, Jesus encountered no less than five
situations involving Satan or evil spirits. One third
of chapter 3 deals with the commonplace mani-
festation of demons, and half of chapter 5 is used
to describe the classic case of the demoniac of the
Gadarenes (also called Gerasenes). Wherever Jesus

went, "unclean" or evil spirits and their chief ruler, Satan, lurk not far from the action.

No doubt this world is filled with devils, as Martin Luther wrote. When the incarnate Son of God, filled with the Holy Spirit, moved in righteous power through the countryside of Galilee and Judea, the demons began to manifest themselves. Without question, the Spirit is moving in greater power in our day than He has for centuries, and the demons are again stirred up. We can learn how to deal with these devils by observing Jesus.

Jesus Encountered Demons Indirectly

The spiritual warfare that raged around Jesus was evident even before He was born. Matthew wrote of how King Herod became increasingly alarmed over reports that a new king was to be born in his realm. When the magi from the East came asking how they might find *"He that is born King of the Jews"* (Matt. 2:2), Herod told them to keep him informed. He meant later to do away with this one he feared would take his throne. Upon discovering he had been tricked, that the wise men were not going to return to give him word, Herod ordered soldiers to fall upon Bethlehem and destroy all male infants two years of age and younger.

This extraordinary measure was not the action of a reasonable man! Far from it. Herod was

inspired by the devil to commit such slaughter. Jesus was spared, of course, because an angel had warned Mary and Joseph to flee into Egypt for a time.

The conflict with Satan was further demonstrated in Nazareth, where Jesus lived for thirty years. The townspeople had watched this son of Joseph grow into manhood. They had not heard Him blaspheme, curse, or hurt anyone. Yet when He returned to Nazareth and spoke in the temple (see Luke 4:16–32), they flew into a rage, seized Him and *"led him unto the brow of the hill whereon their city was built, that they might cast him down headlong"* (v. 29). Why would normal people attempt to kill a good, kind fellow citizen? It was abnormal. It was the devil seeking to destroy Him before His time.

We find this also with the demoniac of Gadara, the man who had a legion of devils in him. (See Mark 5:1–20.) According to the Bible, everyone was afraid of the man—they even feared to pass that way. Strangers and visitors took another road because of this wild man. When Jesus came by, this demoniac roared out against Him. He wanted to destroy Jesus. But Jesus stood before him and asked, *"What is thy name?"* (v. 9). When the spirits identified themselves as *"Legion: for we are many"* (v. 9), Jesus commanded them to come out.

Another indirect encounter with the Prince of Darkness happened when Jesus was asleep in the boat on the Sea of Galilee. A storm arose abnormally fast. The Scripture says it came up suddenly. The devil has some control over the elements, as we learn from the book of Job, and while Jesus slept, Satan tried to dump the boat to the bottom of the sea. No doubt the devil thought that if he could attack Jesus in an indirect way, he could destroy Him. But of course, his attempt failed; the disciples woke Jesus, He rebuked the storm, and a great calm came over the waters.

The devil also sought to destroy Jesus through the hatred and cunning of religious leaders. I do not believe those priests and Pharisees were normally men of hate. Something came upon them. It began with pride. They thought, "Now, if this Jesus stays around He is going to steal our prestige. We have to get rid of Him!"

The devil helped them right up to the point of murdering Jesus.

Satan also attacked Jesus indirectly through Judas, who betrayed our Lord. Luke records that *"then entered Satan into Judas"* (Luke 22:3). Judas was not Jesus' real enemy; the devil was using Judas. Avoiding a face-to-face confrontation, he chose rather to try to destroy Jesus by deceit.

The Direct Confrontations

The best example of direct conflict between Satan and Jesus is the wilderness temptation.

Matthew and Luke both record this in detail. (See Matthew 4:1–11 and Luke 4:1–14.)

The devil came to Jesus when He was alone, preparing for His earthly ministry. For forty days He had prayed and fasted, and His body was weak. The devil thought this would be Jesus' weakest moment. He did not know that although a fasting person's *flesh* may lack strength, his *spirit* can be stronger than ever.

Satan first approached Jesus in the area of his fleshly appetite. "There is a stone," he said. "If you are God, turn it into bread."

Satan knew Jesus was God. After all, Jesus had made him. He knew Jesus was his Creator. But the devil is a deceiver and a liar. He said, "If you are the Son of God...."

Jesus answered, *"It is written, Man shall not live by bread alone, but by every word that proceedeth out of the mouth of God"* (Matt. 4:4). He stood upon the Word of God, quoting to the devil a passage from the Old Testament and thus setting a pattern and example for you and me. We must answer satanic attacks, not with our intelligence, nor our feelings, but with God's Word. Jesus won the first round of this temptation, and so will we when we use the Word of God.

Next, Satan tried to appeal to Jesus' soul. Taking Him to the highest point of the temple, he whispered in His ear, "Now, listen, You are trying to be an evangelist. But You haven't had Your name in the *Jerusalem Post* yet. Nobody has written a feature story about You. You are just a nobody. But now, jump off this temple right into the main street of Jerusalem and say, 'I jumped seventy-two feet here and was not hurt!' Then everybody will praise You and the writers of the *Jerusalem Post* will run out and write a story about You. You need some publicity so that everybody will know about You."

Don't think the devil is not clever. He is. But Jesus answered immediately, *"It is written again, Thou shalt not tempt the Lord thy God"* (Matt. 4:7).

We must never believe the devil. We must not tempt God. What the devil said in Matthew 4:6 was true. (He was actually quoting Psalm 91:11–12 with a key phrase conveniently omitted!) If Jesus *had* fallen down, the angels *would* have taken care of Him. But Jesus said something greater: *"Thou shalt not tempt the Lord thy God."*

Occasionally a magazine or newspaper will carry a story about people who handle snakes as a part of their religion. I lived for a time in the jungle, and deadly snakes were all around me. But I think it would have been opening myself to the devil's harm to have taken one of them up in my arms. I have eaten things that were poisonous and God has healed me because I did not know they were poisonous. Jesus said, *"Thou shalt not tempt...."*

The devil had one more trick up his sleeve— his master stroke. He asked Jesus to simply bow down and worship him. Satan promised Him *"all the kingdoms of the world, and the glory of them"* (Matt. 4:8), but Jesus neither yielded nor bowed.

Jesus had come to earth for the very purpose of reclaiming mankind for His heavenly Father. But with this third temptation, Satan didn't intend to grant what he was offering, and Jesus knew that. It was an attractive shortcut, another of the devil's lies. Jesus answered, *"Get thee hence, Satan: for it is written..."* (v. 10), and the devil left Him—for a time.

Satan's Three Appeals

Satan tempted Jesus along three lines, and he comes to us in these same three ways. His appeals seem attractive. They seem natural. They are pitched toward man's instinctive desire for self-preservation, self-adulation, and self-achievement. Watch out!

Jesus in Action

The Lord Jesus identified demon spirits. He recognized some as deaf spirits. He identified dumbness, infirmities, and wildness. Christ knew the number of demons a person had; He could bring out one or He could bring out a thousand. He cast out seven demons from Mary Magdalene. The number had no relationship to the deliverance. When He spoke the word, the demons had to go, and the people were set free.

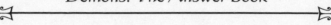
It is worth particular notice that when He commanded Satan to leave, the devil obeyed. Satan had to bow to the greater authority. When you or I command the devil to go in the name of Jesus, he must obey us too. We have that authority.

From modern films and books on the occult and from rites within certain historic denominations, we might conclude that the exorcism of devils is something complex, and that it is for the select few. However, when we turn to the Bible, we see the opposite is true. Jesus rarely spent more than a few minutes setting a person free. Usually all He had to do was issue an authoritative command.

In Matthew 9:32–33, some men brought to Him a *"dumb man possessed with a devil"* (v. 32). The next verse says, *"And when the devil was cast out, the dumb spake"* (v. 33). On another day, *"Then was brought unto him one possessed with a devil, blind, and dumb"* (Matt. 12:22). Matthew simply said that Jesus healed him, restoring both the man's sight and speech.

Following the Transfiguration, Jesus returned to the foot of the mountain to find His disciples defeated and confused. They told Him that a man had brought them his son, *"a lunatic, and sore vexed"* (Matt. 17:15). They didn't have the faith to set him free. According to Matthew's account, Jesus immediately *"rebuked the devil; and he departed out of him: and the child was cured from that very hour"* (v. 18). True, Jesus did emphasize to them the extreme importance of prayer and fasting (v. 21), but the point is that He did not engage in lengthy analysis or ritual. He exercised His rightful dominion and set the boy free.

Our Example

This is an example to the church today. Jesus took authority, commanded demons to leave, and did not waste a lot of time doing it. We are to do the same. He commissioned the church, saying, *"And these signs shall follow them that believe; In my name shall they cast out devils"* (Mark 16:17). Certainly we must be clean vessels. Our hearts must be washed continually by obeying His Word. We must confess all known sin and constantly recognize our position as "under the blood of Jesus." And when we walk in this way, we need simply to command the evil spirits to come out by faith, and they will obey.

Jesus confronted demon power. He did not ignore it. He did not stand off from it. He was not afraid of it. Now we are the voice of Jesus upon this earth. We are the hands and feet of Jesus. We must be ready to carry on His ministry and cast out devils. There was never a time when it was needed so much as now.

Someone asks, "Where are the devils Jesus cast out?" They are not in prison or in hell, as some imagine. The demons Jesus cast out two thousand years ago are in the void of space, or some wilderness, or they are living in some person today.

They seek to indwell human beings, as I found out when I first attempted missionary work in the island of Java, among unreached people dwelling in spiritual darkness. But these demons are not confined to the islands of the sea. Look around you and be convinced. Our work is cut out for us.

4
How I Learned to
Cast Out Demons

❦———————————————❧

Behold how many thousands still are lying,
Bound in the darksome prison house of sin,
With none to tell them of the Savior's dying
Or of the life He died for them to win.

—Mary Ann Thomson, "O Zion, Haste"

Although I was raised in a Full Gospel church, I do not remember hearing much preaching on deliverance from demon power. I cannot remember ever hearing a whole sermon on the devil, his reality, and his works. If they talked about him they called him "Ol' Slewfoot" and said he had horns and a tail. And if they rebuked the devil, they demanded he go back to hell, when in fact he is not in hell and never has been. This would seem highly unusual today, but it also would have been highly unusual then for the preacher to give a full sermon about demons.

In my early twenties I joined Howard Carter of London, and we traveled for years through many countries teaching and evangelizing. We spent three months in Java, Indonesia, where I had my first encounter with a demon-possessed person. She was a young twelve- or thirteen-year-old girl seated on the front row in a service where I was to minister.

During the song service she slipped off the pew and began to writhe on the floor like a snake. A repulsive, green foam oozed from her mouth. She looked terrible, and I felt terrible. However, the Javanese minister paid no attention and went on with the service.

When I rose to speak, something within me stirred. I was deeply indignant. Although I had had no experience with a thing like this, I said firmly, "Get back on that seat."

The Indonesian girl did not understand English, but evidently the devil within her did. Instantly she returned to her seat and remained there motionless for some forty minutes while I preached. Afterward, I prayed at the pulpit for her deliverance in the name of the Lord Jesus Christ. There was no struggle. She was instantly healed. Evidently, at my first words from the pulpit, the devil knew I (through Christ) possessed authority over him.

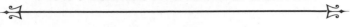

While walking into a church in another part of Indonesia, I was approached by a woman who looked at me and said, "You have a black angel in you, and I have a white angel in me."

God's power moved within me and, rather than walking on toward the pulpit, I immediately said to her, "No, you have a black angel in you, who is the devil. I have a white angel in me, the Lord Jesus Christ. And my angel being the stronger, I command this black angel to come out of you, and that you be free."

The woman instantly went into a kind of convulsion; after a few moments she became as normal as she had ever been. From that moment she was free. She confessed that she had been under the spell of a witch doctor for many years. Now Christ had set her free.

I was not taught this kind of ministry. I had read no books on the subject, except the Bible, but when I met the adversary, the Spirit within me was moved and my heart went out to the afflicted to assist them and bring them back to health.

Christ in the Conflict

As we ministered throughout the island of Java, I encountered the devil a number of times. The greatest thing I learned was that I was not personally in the conflict. It was Christ *in me*. Also, it was not the *person* who caused the battle, but the *devil* within him or her.

I discovered there was no reason to fear. I found that although they would scream and tear themselves, they did not seek to harm me or touch me. I was perfectly safe in exorcising demons. I found in most cases that the demons wanted to run away and avoid confronting me. They would often say, "We are not here; we are gone. Leave us alone." They do not tell the truth.

My Gibraltar

As I sought to confirm this ministry by the Word of God, the Great Commission of our Lord Jesus (Mark 16:15–18) in which He commanded his disciples to cast out devils became my Gibraltar.

It seems that almost every day I receive telephone calls from someone in America who is combating an evil spirit and is seeking help. Almost every day letters come to me from those who are tormented by the devil. After I appeared as a guest of Pat Robertson on *The 700 Club,* I received some 2,500 letters from listeners—most of them inquiring about deliverance.

These people needed deliverance. Philosophy cannot set them free. Pastoral counseling cannot deliver them. Psychiatry cannot deliver them. A psychiatrist from Chattanooga once brought four of his patients with him to my office. He had not been able to effect a cure, and he wanted me to lay hands on them and pray for them.

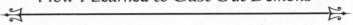

The church has tried to taboo the ministry of exorcising evil spirits. Ministers have tried to turn their backs on the situation and have committed sick people to mental institutions in order to forget them. Yet there is an ever-growing need for the ministry of setting people free in the Spirit.

Those who lead the army of Jesus Christ must not simply be able to pray for the sick, but they must also be able to reach into the spirit of man and set him free from evil, breaking the powers of Satan in his spirit and mind. Yet before they can do that, they must know how to discern the spirits and recognize their presence.

5
Where Satan Dwells

Leave no unguarded place,
no weakness of the soul;
Take every virtue, every grace,
and fortify the whole.
From strength to strength go on,
wrestle and fight and pray;
Tread all the powers of darkness down,
And win the well-fought day.

—Charles Wesley,
"Soldiers of Christ, Arise"

One cannot hope to deal with the subject of demon power without expecting one question above all others: Can a Christian have a demon? Can an evil spirit enter in and possess a believer?

The controversy on this issue rages around a theory of recognition and definition. Who is a Christian? What can happen in his life?

The Bible emphatically states in James 4:7, *"Resist the devil, and he will flee from you."* This is the position of the born-again believer. Jesus Christ, in His ultimate commission to the church, said, *"In my name shall they cast out devils"* (Mark 16:17).

The Christian should not fear the devil; he should cast him out, dethrone him, exorcise him.

However, a person who identifies himself or herself as a Christian and goes to fortune-tellers, plays the Ouija board, and depends on horoscopes for guidance is an open door for the entrance of the evil one. Almost every worshipper and high priest of witchcraft in Brazil will tell you he is a Christian. This is what I mean by definition. The apostle Paul had no fear of demons or their power, but the sons of Sceva did. (See Acts 19:13–17.)

We deal with this further in a later chapter, but first we should consider the habitations of devils about which there is no dispute. Satan himself, and the demons that serve him, inhabit the nations of this world and seek to dominate them. He is called *"the god of this world"* (2 Cor. 4:4) for good reason. His spirits, which no one can number, have their residence in the atmosphere of the planet Earth. His presence can almost be seen and felt in the places of this world where the Gospel of Jesus Christ has not entered to challenge his ground.

The Bible says ancient Babylon had become *"the habitation of devils, and the hold of every foul spirit"* (Rev. 18:2). In Isaiah's descriptive account of the devil's origin (Isaiah 14:12–19), the devil is accused of having "weakened the nations" (v. 12). Lucifer, as he is called in this passage, *"made the earth to tremble, that did shake kingdoms"* (v. 16).

Satan's Initial Desire

Satan desired to be like the Creator. His chief ambition was to replace God in heaven. To do this, he initiated a rebellion against God in the heavens and continued to carry it out when he was cast down to earth before the Creation. Man's history from the beginning until now is laced with conflicts and crises in which the devil is "weakening the kingdoms" by war, pestilence, famine, moral degradation, and every conceivable means.

When viewing our modern world it is not difficult to illustrate how the devil causes the earth to tremble. The recent history of Auschwitz, the Nazi blitz, and the mass purges under Stalin are already fading in the light of more current atrocities.

Cambodia

We are told by none other than Mr. Chang Song, the minister of information in the former Cambodian regime, that from 1975 to 1978 some 2.3 million citizens of that "gentle land" were killed. That is one third of the nation's population!

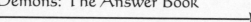

Godless Khmer Rouge armies enforced a total evacuation of Cambodia's leading cities when they came to power. The land resembles a wilderness more than the garden it once was. But while the Khmer appear to be the murderers there, the *real* murderer is Lucifer. Isaiah prophesied of Lucifer that he *"made the world as a wilderness, and destroyed the cities thereof"* (Isa. 14:17).

Uganda

Nightmare was the only word befitting the state of that African republic when Idi Amin seized power over its ten million people.

A Ugandan leaving the country said,

It is no good. It is Amin himself. He has a mental problem and you never know when you will die....The army can do nothing....Now they are as frightened of him [Amin] as the civilians; he has killed ruthlessly there....Who kills for him? Youngsters he has chosen and trained....they kill anyone, anywhere, for fun, and they murder at his direction. [1]

I do not believe Amin could have done what he did in that country—with the flow of blood there—had he not been possessed by the devil. Author Gwyn himself attributes the "indiscriminate killing" to "something that cannot be fully explained by Amin's own pathological example and influence." Gwyn links the use of magic and witchcraft with the killings. "It is true," he says, "that Amin is relying heavily on magic." He adds, "It is often said of these troops that 'their eyes have gone mad with blood, and magic is at work.'"

I am reminded of Adolf Hitler and Benito Mussolini. It is said that Mussolini declared, "I would shake hands with the devil if he would help me get the desire of my heart." Much of his generation trembled before that man's exaggerations. No one realized he had already shaken hands with Satan!

Christian missionaries have long been acquainted with the fact that certain nations are uniquely the devil's territory. Until recent years the majority of stories of demon possession, voodoo, exorcism, and witchcraft came from the countries of Asia, Latin America, Africa, and various islands.

Indonesia

Indonesia was the first non-Christian country I ministered in when, as a twenty-one-year-old evangelist, I began preaching overseas. In the three months I was there, and in all my travels since, I have never seen as much demon power and as many witch doctors anywhere as I did in Indonesia.

India

No country saddens my heart like India. For many years the nations of the West have been trying to help India get on her feet and develop the capability to feed her teeming masses. But it is still a losing battle. I believe that until India turns away from her three-thousand-year-old worship of three hundred million idols and turns to the living God, her problems will never be solved. She is a nation under the dominion of the devil.

Tibet

Just across India's northern border is Tibet, an ancient and isolated land where Satan has reigned supreme for ages. With the Rev. Howard Carter, I traveled into Tibet during the 1930s. We could feel the strange power of the devil there. The dirt, filth, and stench were almost overpowering. Characteristic of the Lamaist temples of this mountain kingdom are the hundreds of grotesque idols—actually demon idols—that are sculpted into the interior walls of the temples.

During our stay there we slept in the heathen temples (there was no other place to sleep) and listened to strange stories of demon power. One missionary told us he had witnessed a Tibetan monk, in a frenzy of mystic power, twist a steel sword so that it resembled a corkscrew.

Guyana

In November 1978, at Jonestown, Guyana, the leader of the People's Temple, Jim Jones, very definitely surrendered his spirit and intelligence to the devil and committed one of the greatest atrocities in history.

America

Demon power has dominated nations in the past, and it threatens to do so in America today. Witchcraft, the occult, and sensual evil has never been as blatant in America as it is right now. We are in a time when the devil is seeking to conquer America. If our generation fails to take authority over the devil and his demons, our children and their children could well live in a country that is tyrannized by a demon-possessed dictator, an Adolf Hitler or a Josef Stalin.

The Lord Jesus Christ, when He appeared to John on the isle of Patmos, issued a message for the churches in seven key cities of Asia. Nothing could more graphically demonstrate the importance He placed on the cities of the world. And Satan like-wise chooses to operate from key cities.

Pergamos was one of those cities named by our Lord. *"I know thy works and where thou dwellest,"* He said to the church in Pergamos,

> *Even where Satan's seat is: and thou holdest fast my name, and hast not denied my faith, even in those days wherein Antipas was my faithful martyr, who was slain among you, **where Satan dwelleth**.*
> (Rev. 2:13, emphasis added)

Ancient Babylon was a city under Satan's control, as we shall see. Some students of sorcery have traced witchcraft back to this great metropolitan center of the old world.

Heavenly Conflict

The prophet Daniel, in exile in Babylon, received a vision (Daniel 9 and 10) that explained why he had not received an answer to his prayers of more than three weeks in duration (Dan. 10:2). An angel appeared to him, informing him that one known as *"the prince of the kingdom of Persia"* (v. 13) had obstructed Daniel's petitions. The angel said that, as soon as he left Daniel, he (the angel) would again have to fight this spirit and another called *"the prince of Grecia"* (v. 20), but that *"Michael your prince"* (v. 21) would aid him in this battle. What we see here is the heavenly conflict between Satan's angels (or demons) and God's hosts. The princes of Persia and Grecia were undoubtedly high officers in the devil's world dominion.

The Devil Has Not Changed

The devil was very real to Martin Luther, and a letter the Reformer wrote in 1524 contains the telling line: "I am having a terrible time with the Satan of Alstedt [a Saxon town]." [2]

Certain cities today are the devil's dwelling places. One of the most depressing cities in the world is Calcutta, a city named for a female goddess. Cali, the ugly, glary-eyed idol in temples there, receives worship and blood sacrifice.

A missionary told me once that when he delivered an Indian woman possessed of a demon, the evil spirit told him, "I am from Cali in Cal-cutta."

When the missionary asked the spirit how it had entered the woman, it answered, "She worshipped in our temple in Calcutta." The missionary replied, "Come out of her, in Jesus' name," and it came out, weeping loudly and saying, "Now I must journey back to Calcutta to find somebody else in whom to live."

Gone to the Devil

Evil spirits seem to be drawn to cities. Since they apparently are not satisfied until they dwell within a human body, they congregate in places where humans are numerous. Their strength is most evident in cities that, for some reason, have little of the light of the Gospel. Paris, New York City, Hollywood—these cities I believe are under the devil's ruling power.

It is said that a Frenchman can live all his life in a small French town or on a farm and remain pure and upright, but give him two days in Paris and he will lose his virtue. New York City does that to countless young people every year—people who go there looking for life at its best. A spirit of greed is in control of that great metropolis, and if our eyes were only able to see them, we would observe the hoards of evil spirits that make this city their dwelling place.

We should weep over our cities, as Jesus did for Jerusalem, lest they become throne rooms for Satan. One reason evil becomes concentrated in big cities is because they are full of soothsayers, crystal-gazers, fortune-tellers, spiritualist media, and cults of all kinds.

Man and Animal Life— The Devil's Habitations

Beasts may be possessed by demons also. Jesus encountered this phenomenon when, in the well-known case of the Gadarene demoniac (see Matthew 8:28–32), he sent the legion of spirits into a nearby herd of swine. These pigs immediately became insane and were filled with a suicidal spirit abnormal to animals. They raced into the sea and were drowned.

A generation or two ago, when Americans had a much closer relationship with animals, certain beasts often became possessed. I have seen horses that went berserk and had to be put to death. Their owners called them "mad horses." Dogs also would become suddenly abnormal and vicious.

Animals are very conscious of the presence of demons. When evil power lurks, they become nervous and sometimes noisy. On the other hand, they respond to love, tenderness, and kind words. By receiving affection, they may be protected from evil powers.

Parts of the human body can be habitations
of devils. Several times our Lord cast out spirits
of deafness and dumbness from people. He also
cast out spirits of "infirmity" (weakness). Francis
MacNutt says that, in his experience, the spirit of
infirmity will even move from one part of the body
to another—seeking to avoid giving up its place in
a person's body—when a Christian is commanding it to leave. Evidently, an evil spirit takes over a
certain part of the body and does not relinquish it
until someone rebukes it with divine authority.

Just as the Holy Spirit seeks to reside fully in
and have control over a Christian's life, evil spirits
also seek complete possession. Jesus encountered
this immediately upon beginning His ministry. A
person reading the first few chapters of Mark's gospel
will be amazed at how often Jesus met people who
needed deliverance from demons. The writers of the
Synoptic Gospels describe these encounters matter-
of-factly, since they were common occurrences. (See
Luke 4:33; 4:41; 8:2; 9:1; Matthew 12:22; Mark 1:23–27,
32–34, 39; 3:11, 22–23).

The most revealing deliverance in the Bible is
the healing of the demoniac of Gadara (already
mentioned several times). The evil spirits in this
wretched man told Jesus they were *"Legion"* (Mark
5:9); that is, they numbered between two and five
thousand! But they all obediently left the Gadarene
at Jesus' command, never to torment the man
again.

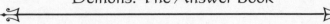

Many—even preachers and learned religious professors—try to explain away demon possession today. They attribute disorders and illnesses to mental illness or physical causes. In many cases I do not dispute that, but this does not discount the primal cause for these often terrible conditions: Evil spirits are oppressing and possessing hundreds of thousands of people today. They do not need medicine or psychoanalysis; they need a simple prayer offered on their behalf by one of Christ's believing children who will claim authority over spirits that have usurped God's place of honor and blessing.

Dramatic Deliverances!

A few years ago a woman traveled all the way from New Mexico to our church in South Bend, Indiana, to be delivered of evil spirits. She was in her forties, and the demons had been so strong in her that she had not been able to eat at the table with her husband for more than twenty years. She had a terrible pain in her abdomen and was a social outcast. This lady came to me in desperate straits, unable to live any longer, she felt, if she did not gain relief.

We documented this deliverance and later made a recording ("And the Demon Answered Back") of the actual sounds of the demons within her. She was not easily set free. It took more than one of us agreeing in prayer, with fasting, to take authority. But she was set free.

In 1963 our church hosted Arlindo Barbosa de Oliviera of Brazil and sponsored a tour of forty American cities where he gave testimony of his deliverance from evil spirits. People across the country can still remember Arlindo relating how more than five hundred devils possessed him at one time. He knew their names and had worshipped them in different ways.

He told me that at times he used to lie in a trance in the government office in Brasilia where he worked and receive information psychically about secrets behind closed doors in Washington. He said that at other times the spirits would cause him to eat and drink ground glass without doing himself any harm. One of the demons desired strong drink, and Arlindo drank certain types of wine when this devil was active in him. A Methodist missionary set him free, and he has been serving God ever since.

The Devil Is Real

I did not need Arlindo to prove to me that demons exist today and that they are always seeking to enter human bodies. The Christian has nothing to fear, for *"greater is he that is in you, than he that is in the world"* (1 John 4:4). But we do have to be alert. When you play with fire, you can get burned. And if you carelessly go into Satan's territory, you can open yourself up to his evil work.

Notes

1. David Gwyn, *Idi Amin: Death-Light of Africa* (Boston: Little, Brown & Co., 1977), p. 130.

2. Roland Bainton, *Here I Stand* (Nashville: Abingdon, 1951), p. 263.

6
Proven Ways to Recognize Demon Power

Humanity is preparing itself to yield to demon
influences in a way that has not prevailed
in modern time.

—Wilbur M. Smith [1]

In the late 1950s I wrote that we are living
through the greatest spiritual crisis in two
thousand years and that in this crisis angels
and demons will be known to man in an unprec-
edented manner. "Christians will find angels sup-
porting and succoring them," I said. "There will be
more demon activity, more people oppressed and
possessed, than the world has ever known."

This was before the revival of the occult had reached the proportions it has today in America. The drug trafficking and pornographic publishing rackets, although they were forces to reckon with, were not directly affecting millions of young lives as they are now. Films like *The Exorcist* and *The Omen* were no more than dreams in the minds of a few writers.

What has happened? Is it only for box-office profits and newsstand sales that today's generation is inundated with details about the demonic? Or is there something sinister, real, and incomparably evil out there?

In crises of the past, an unusual display of angelic power was accompanied by extraordinary activity of demons. Such phenomena were well documented in the lifetime of Jesus Christ. More angels were in evidence from the time of His announced birth until His ascension than in the entire four thousand years of Old Testament history. At the same time, demon power was more in evidence during that period than at any previous time.

The Final Crisis?

A great number of Bible-believing Christians are convinced that we are now living in the final crisis of mankind. The irony and tragedy is that the less the church teaches about demon power, the more control Satan takes over society. Half the world is possessed by the devil, and the other half doesn't believe the devil exists—of course, the devil sees to it the two never meet!

In recent years, a half-dozen excellent books about the devil and demon power, written from conservative evangelical viewpoints, have been published. I take this as an encouraging sign that the Lord is preparing His people to do battle in these last days. In order that we will not be jousting at windmills and seeking demons in every house and home, in this chapter I will point out how demon power may be recognized in society today.

Crime

I begin with crime for obvious reasons. Demonic power can be seen more easily and more often in crimes against persons, property, and society than anywhere else.

This comes as no surprise to those who know the Bible. Jesus said the devil is a *"thief"* whose threefold work is *"to steal, and to kill, and to destroy"* (John 10:10). To the unbelieving Jews of His generation, Jesus said,

> *You are of your father the devil, and your will is to do your father's desires. He was a murderer from the beginning, and has nothing to do with the truth....When he lies, he speaks according to his own nature, for he is a liar and the father of lies.* (John 8:44 RSV)

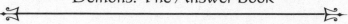

Writing under divine inspiration, Isaiah described the conditions existing in his day—conditions that are still true today.

> *For your hands are defiled with blood and your fingers with iniquity; your lips have spoken lies, your tongue mutters wickedness. No one enters suit justly, no one goes to law honestly; they rely on empty pleas, they speak lies, they conceive mischief and bring forth iniquity.* (Isa. 59:3–4 RSV)

Anyone who considers the immensity of crime in America today is compelled to admit that demons are a driving force. When Jesus declared that in the last days *"iniquity shall abound"* (Matt. 24:12), He was speaking in terms broader than man's inhumanity to man. Satan, knowing his time is short, has unleashed his demon forces to do violence and take peace from the earth.

Almost every day newspapers and news magazines report crimes that defy description—deeds that can only be accounted for through demonic power. A mother strangles her little child to death and later confesses to police, "A voice told me to do it." The voice of the devil told her to destroy her child.

The big cities of America have become unsafe; quite a few have been terrorized by one or more madmen. Boston has had its "Strangler," Los Angeles its Manson murders and the "Hillside Strangler," and New York its "Son of Sam" (the .44-caliber killer). The convicted "Son of Sam" slayer testified in court that, at the command of a dog, he went out to murder young women in New York City in 1977 and 1978.

During a recent crusade in Manila, I again visited Dr. Mariano Lara at Bilibid prison. After a friendly greeting, he said, "Mr. Sumrall, I surely wish you had been here a day earlier." When I asked why, he took me to the morgue and showed me the mutilated bodies of two small children.

He explained that the parents of these children had come home from a spiritist meeting under a spell and imagined the children were actually devils. The parents grabbed their young son and daughter and stuck objects down their throats, up their noses, and in their eyes and ears. The children screamed in pain until they died. When police arrived the parents said they had found two devils in their house.

"But these are your own children," the police said.

"No," the parents insisted. "We found two evil spirits in our house and sought to subdue them."

The illicit and criminal use of drugs has contributed to the current dramatic rise in all kinds of crime. The wide use of hallucinogenic drugs that created the "beat generation" and later spawned the hippie cult promised grand benefits. Beyond the immediate sensation of carefree ecstasy, there were new horizons for the soul, expansion of the consciousness, and contact with eternity. But it was all a lie of the devil. True, these drugs did grant immediate breakthroughs, but with immeasurable harm to the users.

Strangely, the use of drugs and heavy addiction continues despite intensive educational programs by the government, the church, the media, and such Christian groups as Teen Challenge. Politicians have compromised themselves so much that many can no longer distinguish right from wrong; they continue to yield to pressure to legalize "less harmful" drugs. (Indeed, with our nation's indefensibly lax attitude toward alcohol and tobacco, it makes poor logic to mount a campaign against the availability of marijuana, heroin, and cocaine.)

A CBS *Sixty Minutes* program showed the unpredictable and destructive effects of a drug known as PCP. Two young men interviewed on the show told grisly tales of murders they committed while high on PCP. Satan has tremendous power to tempt man with drugs, and in our day this has become a fearful weapon. The whole scene—the drug substances and their empty claims, together with society's inability to control them—is demonic in origin. As we approach the end of the age, crimes will become more ghastly and the human heart will become harder.

Moral Sins

While it is true that people have always been morally delinquent, we are approaching a time when the world will be under fierce attack by immoral spirits. We can expect homes in America to continue to fall apart. At the pace the devil is working now, there soon will not be many decent homes left—home life as we have known it in the past. People will live on an animal level, changing homes every night. Satan is determined to "Hollywoodize" the homes of America.

Adultery is a spirit. Men have told me, "I would give anything in the world if I could quit my immoral life, but I cannot." Immorality has a strange hold on them. Such a person is possessed with a spirit of adultery.

I do not believe statistics that suggest one of every ten Americans is homosexual. Three decades ago the Kinsey Report found that "four percent of all men and significantly fewer women are homosexual throughout their lives...that figure is considered too high by most sociologists. The more recent Hunt study...put the incidence among men at three percent, of which perhaps one percent are openly active in a gay community." [2] Yet the so-called "gay" community is large, more visible, and apparently on the increase.

I believe that sodomy is a spirit. It is unnatural for a man to have sexual relations with another man, or a woman with a woman. It must be from an evil spirit. This horrible sin is causing consternation throughout the world. In my ministry I have prayed for a number of perverts, and they have told me of the craving and compulsion that keeps them bound. They recognize it is from the spirit world.

The Lord Jesus Christ said, *"As it was in the days of Lot...even thus shall it be in the day when the Son of man is revealed"* (Luke 17:28, 30). In Lot's day, sodomy was the prevailing sin, and it is rapidly becoming so in our day. God hates it no less today than He did in Lot's day when He brought awful judgment upon them. Those who indulge in it are demon-possessed, I believe, and need divine deliverance. Psychiatry cannot deliver a person; only the power of Christ can set him free.

The church has been infiltrated with this spirit of sodomy. In recent years we have witnessed a pitiful thing—major denominations spending large sums of people's tithes and gifts to prepare position reports on homosexuality. I approve of efforts we in the church can make to communicate an open, compassionate, loving attitude toward homosexuals as persons, but it should be very clear that the Bible condemns the spirit and practice of homosexuality. That there is now a Metropolitan Community Church in Los Angeles with twenty thousand professed homosexuals as members is but one example of the fulfillment of Paul's writing in Romans 1. He showed that when man would not believe the light of divine revelation and obey the Gospel,

> *God gave them up in the lusts of their hearts to impurity, to the dishonoring of their bodies among themselves...to dishonorable passions. Their women exchanged natural relations for unnatural, and the men likewise gave up natural relations with women and were consumed with passion for one another, men committing shameless acts with men and receiving in their own persons the due penalty for their error.*
>
> (Rom. 1:24, 26–27 RSV)

Pornography and obscene movies are evils out of the pit of hell. Perhaps enough has been written of them to make their nature clear. But the "respectable" moral sins of greed (about which I will say more), racial bigotry, affluent apathy toward the poor, and dependence upon military force and power instead of God are also symptomatic of an evil spirit of the age.

Love of Money

Writing to the Colossian church, Paul warned against covetousness or greed, which he equated with idolatry (Col. 3:5). And in 1 Corinthians he equated idols with demons (1 Cor. 10:20). Insatiable covetousness, the love and lust for money, is without question a spirit; it is another area in which we may expect increased demon power in the days ahead.

The Bible says *"the love of money is the root of all evil"* (1 Tim. 6:10). Someone may say, "I cannot see demon power in the area of money." But many people are addicted to money; greed is as much a narcotic to them as heroin is to the dope addict. And it is of the devil. Because of money, people abuse their families, cheat and lie, and sell their reputations as well as their bodies and souls. In fact, almost every evil in the world can be traced to the love and lust for money. It breaks up homes, causes people to rob and kill, and destroys the good things of life.

Too many Americans have allowed the dollar to become their master. A man came to my office in South Bend and asked if he could talk with me about his marital problems. He had heard me preach on the radio. He told me the story of his shattered marriage.

"I have worked like a slave all my life," he said. "For a number of years I worked at two jobs—sixteen hours a day. I built a beautiful home in South Bend and a cottage at the lake. I have a late-model car. I thought I was doing all this for my wife. I thought she wanted it, too. But one day while I was at work, a salesman came to my house. My wife let him demonstrate a sweeper and before he left they had committed adultery. Taking advantage of my absence, he returned to my home time and again, and quite often the two of them would go out to the lake cottage and commit sin."

He sobbed out his story, pausing momentarily to control his emotions.

"I am so brokenhearted that I don't know what to do," he continued. "I didn't believe it could happen to me. I see now that if I had not been so greedy for money and for material things, I would still have my wife. I put money first and her second. I was never as loving as I should have been. Now I have lost my wife, for she has left me for this other man. She told me she would rather live in a one-room apartment with someone who loved her than with an old miser who worked sixteen hours a day. I tried to tell her I was doing all this just for her, but she laughed at me and said she never got any of it."

The love of money can and does become an evil spirit. It can cause a man in New York to steal a million dollars in the stock market, only to confess later, "Why did I ever do it?" He did it because he was possessed with a spirit and lost control of his life.

In Joseph Borkin's book, *The Corrupt Judge* (Clarkson N. Potter, 1962), a Washington attorney tells of three highly respected federal judges in New York and Pennsylvania who, over a period of twenty years, bought and sold "justice" in local bankruptcy and embezzlement cases.

In the high reaches of the federal judiciary, one of the judges attempted to build a corporate empire on "loans," "advance payments on contracts," and plain bribes accepted from people appearing before his court of appeals.

Another judge frequently accepted payments of money in rolled-up newspapers in the dark hallway of the federal court building, while a third judge terrorized all the lawyers in his district for twenty years until he was finally caught by the U.S. Department of Justice.

Some public officials are honest and decent, yet corruption of this sort permeates all levels of government, business, and society in America. It threatens to ruin our nation.

Apostasy

The apostle Paul wrote,

Now the Spirit speaketh expressly, that in the latter times some shall depart from the faith, giving heed to seducing spirits, and doctrines of devils.

(1 Tim. 4:1)

The Spirit mentioned here is the Holy Spirit, the third person of the Trinity, who speaks with great emphasis and concern. He has a specific message for the church concerning the *"latter times."* We can be sure that if there ever will be *"latter times,"* they are occurring now.

The Holy Spirit gives His message: "In the latter times some will depart from the faith and allow themselves to be seduced by the subversive doctrines of devils." This departure is called apostasy—"abandonment or renunciation of one's religious faith or allegiance."

No one can depart from something they have not had. These people whom the Holy Spirit identifies know the truth, yet deliberately depart from the faith just as Adam and Eve disobeyed God in the Garden of Eden.

These people are not mere backsliders. God's Word says they give *"heed"*; in other words, they give their whole attention and mind *"to seducing spirits, and doctrines of devils."*

A seducing spirit is a lying spirit, a deceiving spirit. There are many in the world today. *"Doctrines of devils"* means exactly what it says. Satan has now, as he has always had, a doctrine or teaching he proclaims. Satan told Eve she surely would not die if she disobeyed God. Satan asked Christ to worship him. Doctrines of devils will take whomever believes them to hell. Is this being fulfilled today? I believe it is.

I was preaching in the state of Washington and was called to pray for a woman. I walked into her home and spent a few minutes talking to her, but I could not pray. I had a strange feeling that something was wrong. The woman was not ill; it was something more devilish.

She said to me, "Father Divine will be here in a few minutes."

"He will?" I exclaimed. "Then I will stay and see him."

In a few minutes I heard a dog bark from the front porch and an awful presence entered the room. The woman said, "Father's here."

God's anointing came upon me. I laid my hands on the woman and said, "You evil spirit, you lying spirit, come out of her." And she was instantly delivered from the power of the devil. Afterward, the woman confessed this evil spirit had come to her at four every afternoon for a long while and had taken control of her life. She had been a Bible-believing Christian, but had let Satan enter her life.

For every Father Divine or Sun Myung Moon, there are a hundred—perhaps that is too conservative a guess—less prominent false messiahs. Many were once in the true church, but some false doctrine has turned their heads.

In Manila there is a movement called Manalo. The founder, who had been a member of a Christian church, decided he was an angel with a supernatural mission in life. By a strange power he caused people in his services to weep. Before he would ordain anyone to preach to his congregations, the candidate had to have the power to make the entire congregation weep. He built magnificent churches in and around Manila and across the nation. I suppose a million people in the Philippines follow him. They are swayed by his magnetic personality, and they weep as he proclaims himself an angel from heaven.

Before Moon appeared in Korea, a leader named Pak got his start in one of the Christian denominations. Through the power of the devil, he has gathered thousands of people around him. The last time I was there he was selling his bathwater in small bottles, supposedly to heal people when they drank it. He has become an exceedingly wealthy man.

In America too, people in great numbers are being deceived and spiritually seduced by lying demons. I do not wish to appear as controversial, but I do wish to be a revealer of truth. I feel that churches such as the Christian Scientists, the Jehovah's Witnesses, and the Mormons—those who add to the Bible as they wish, and who take from the Bible as they wish—are part of the apostasy of the last days. And I have discovered that when Satan starts anyone in error, he leads him from error to error. Once Satan gets a person on the wrong road, he leads him into damnable doctrines.

Demon Worship

From her birth as a nation, America has sent missionaries to foreign lands to deliver those who were bound in the prison of sin and demonic power. Our missionaries brought life and hope through the Gospel to many people, and set them free. But today, heathen religions are invading America in large numbers. Their "missionaries," if you please, are seeking to convert the "unreached" population of America.

Buddhism, Hinduism, and Islam are growing in our cities. I visited a magnificent Buddhist temple in San Francisco and observed about three hundred Americans studying Buddhism. It is no longer a phenomenon of the West Coast; the devil's religions are making a play for the minds of all our young people, from subtle transcendental meditation to open Satan worship. There have been many magazine stories in recent years on Satan worship in America. This theme occasionally furnishes the backdrop for a television show.

Noted Bible scholar Dr. Wilbur M. Smith wrote, "It is most significant that all specific demon activity referred to after the ascension of our Lord is to be found in relation to the end of this age." [4] From Scripture he concludes we are right in believing that demon activity will be prevalent, powerful, and violent. In the closing days of the age, demons set the stage for the Antichrist, and the chief "props" in this grand deception are religion and demon worship. Jesus told His disciples that *"false Christs and false prophets"* would arise, showing *"signs and wonders, to seduce, if it were possible, even the elect"* (Mark 13:22).

Persistent rejection of truth destroys one's sense of truth and lays a person open to *"deceivableness of unrighteousness"* (2 Thess. 2:10), and to the *"working of Satan with all power and signs and lying wonders"* (v. 9). As already pointed out, it is to be deplored, but expected, that large cities in America have become centers of false cults and demon worship. Heathen priests from India and other lands use the Saturday religion pages of daily newspapers to propagate their doctrine of reincarnation. When false teachers advertise that "the promised one of all religions has come," it is not surprising that confused and deceived men and women flock to such meetings.

An empty and confused soul becomes a sign to the devil, "House to Let," as it were, and Satan and his demons take up the vacancy. (See Luke 11:24–26.) This explains why we are seeing such widespread activity of demons in religion and worship. "As the soul of man becomes increasingly depleted spiritually and the idea of God grows dimmer and dimmer in the souls of men, man's soul becomes, as it were, an undefended fortress into which these evil powers have easy access," said Dr. Smith. "Humanity is preparing itself to yield to demon influences in a way that has not prevailed in modern times." [5]

Inexplicable Cases of Demon Possession

Some people are tormented by the devil and it seems impossible to find any reason for it.

Consider a person injured in an automobile accident. Although the injury was physical, a few months later this person becomes irritable and unbearably antisocial. What was a physical condition ends with an evil spirit. After the accident occurred, the devil moved in through a physical weakness.

Years ago one of my best friends, Go Puan Seng, the owner and publisher of a newspaper in the Philippines, called on me for help. One of his daughters became possessed with evil, and their fine Christian home was thrown into an uproar. This lovely girl lost her loveliness. She would beat the piano rather than play it. She choked the cat until it died and beat her head with her fists until she fell unconscious. Finally she refused to eat altogether. For three months her physician kept her alive with intravenous feeding. She claimed something was in her throat and stomach that would not permit food to enter.

If this case had happened today, her condition would probably be diagnosed as *anorexia nervosa*, about which much has been written in recent years. But the doctor and the family did not know what to do or where to turn. Her father realized that a spirit possessed his daughter.

To test the father's faith, I told him I would fast for two days and then pray for the girl "under one condition," I said. "You prepare a dinner and after I pray for her deliverance, the girl must eat."

Mr. Go was agreeable. "My wife and I will also fast," he said.

For two days I fasted and prayed for God to deliver this girl, and then I returned to their home.

Although no one from the house could see who was at the front gate, the girl screamed when I arrived. "I will not see him," she said, and ran into the basement.

Her father supposed I could not pray for her now, but I was ready. "I have fasted and prayed for two days," I said. "I must pray for her now."

I agreed with him that I would not be offended at anything she would do to me, nor was he to be offended at anything I would ask of her. I walked into the basement to find her. She was standing in a corner, and I went over to speak to her. Suddenly she brandished a knife and tried to strike me with it.

Shaking the knife from her hand, I began to pray. God's mighty power came into the room. Her mother and father were present and the three of us saw visible movements in her stomach as the evil spirit came out.

Instead of having the meal prepared in his own kitchen, Brother Go had arranged for it to be catered. We sat down to a Chinese feast. For the first time in three months, this poor little girl, weighing less than sixty pounds, began to eat. As she ate she said, "Now I am going to die. All my intestines are flat and have not had anything in them for so long."

I turned to her and said, "You are not going to die; you are going to live." I laid my hands on her

and asked God to create the digestive juices needed in her body.

We slowly went through course after course of this dinner. I was seated beside her and put the food on her plate. She turned to me and said, "I feel I am going to vomit. I cannot stand this food in me."

"None of that," I said. "If you become nauseated, you will have to start over again. You must eat."

Following the meal, I took her arm and walked with her in the garden, talking with her about the power of God, the promises of God, and how she must now live for God. With every step she became stronger. She was healed. Great joy returned to the family.

Not all stories end like this. But some years later I was permitted to assist in performing her wedding. She married a fine Chinese student at the University of California. She was a lovely bride; no one would ever dream she once looked anything like the person I found in the basement of her home that morning.

Even in America I have heard of many situations of demon possession that have no explanation. Recently in South Bend, a mother brought her eleven-year-old daughter to me, telling me the girl had become overwhelmed by some kind of evil power. She could no longer attend school, for she

disrupted classes with her fighting and screaming. She would not obey her parents, refusing to
do what they told her. She would sit in the middle
of the floor and throw tantrums. Her parents were
sure it was an evil spirit.

I was asked to pray for her in front of the
church. As I laid my hands on her head she began
screaming, throwing herself about in a violent way.
I commanded the evil spirit to come out of her. She
became subdued, and her mother took her home.

A few weeks later someone came running up to
me as I revisited the church. It was this little girl,
beautiful and normal.

"Are you well?" I asked.

She replied, "I'm so happy."

Her mother told me that her daughter had been
delivered of this evil spirit and her healing had
brought great joy into the home. No one knew why
this thing happened. The only thing the parents
knew was that suddenly everything went wrong
inside their little girl.

Everywhere I go in my travels, I find similar
conditions. It is indeed sad to see people become
victims of satanic depression and obsession. Every
home should be covered by the blood of Christ, for
I know the devil cannot harm the members then. A
Christian has no reason to fear, because *"He that is
in us is greater than he that is in the world"* (1 John 4:4).
However, Christians do need to be aware of the

protecting blood of Christ and of their right to the power and authority of Jesus' name. We are told to rebuke the devil, and he will flee from us.

Every Christian will rejoice on that glorious day when Satan will be bound. (See Revelation 20:1–3.) The deceiver of the nations will cease all his activities. In the meantime, there is one refuge from the lies and deception of the wicked one, and that is Jesus Christ. This is an hour to know you are in Christ, to live for Him, and to win souls for Him.

Notes

1. Dr. Wilbur M. Smith, *World Crisis and the Prophetic Scripture* (Chicago: Moody Press, 1951).

2. Ken Ross, "Gay Rights: The Coming Struggle," *The Nation*, Nov. 19, 1977.

4. Smith, *World Crisis and the Prophetic Scripture*.

5. Ibid.

7
Going to the Devil, Step-by-Step

Yield not to temptation for yielding is sin,
Each vict'ry will help you some other to win;
Fight manfully onward, dark passions subdue,
Look ever to Jesus—He'll carry you through.

—H. R. Palmer, "Yield Not to Temptation"

The devil seldom takes a life all at once. He does it a little at a time, step-by-step. Sometimes he is able to assume complete control rapidly, but usually it is a slow process over a period of weeks, months, or even years.

He is like the proverbial camel who first puts his nose in the Arab's tent, then slowly moves all the way in. The devil is like a cancer—he devours the human personality bit by bit. The steps he uses

93

to destroy human life fall into a definite pattern, which I call the seven steps toward full demon possession.

The steps to possession follow a logical order to a final conclusion. They begin with the smallest amount of demon power and continue until the person is completely overwhelmed. I explain this not to frighten people, but to reveal an antidote that can heal. We must know how the devil attacks and harasses mankind. We also must be confident that Jesus Christ can set us free from anything the devil tries to do. Lucifer hates us because we are the sons and daughters of God. He wants to destroy us, but it is our prerogative to attack and defeat him.

I do not mean to suggest that in every case of demon assault these seven steps, or stages, will be readily evident. On the contrary, there might be some intermediary steps not discussed here. Perhaps in some cases it may even appear that the steps occur in a different order from the progression I have outlined.

Regression

I call the first step of the devil's attack regression. It is a battle against a person's God-given abilities of release and expression. To regress in the human personality is to go backward in spiritual force and power. Men and women are built for progress, advancement, and understanding. When this goes into reverse it is the first warning that negative powers are at work.

A small boy once helped solve a great engineering problem. A bridge was to be constructed across a deep chasm and the engineers could find no way to stretch their heavy cables across the span.

"I can do it," said the lad.

Attaching a cord to the tail of a kite, he let the kite soar over the chasm, carrying the cord to men on the opposite side. Then a rope was tied to the cord and pulled across. The heavy cables were then attached to the rope and stretched into place. First a string, then a rope, then an unbreakable cable.

The devil works in a similar manner. He first binds his victims with a light cord of regression. At this stage the prisoner could easily snap his bonds and be free. Then the evil one adds heavier bonds, until the ropes of oppression are securely in place. It is still possible for the victim to free himself by resisting with all that is within him. But soon the devil adds heavier bonds, until the victim is helplessly bound by the cruel cables of complete demon possession. Then only a fearless servant of God can break the bonds and set the prisoner free by the power and authority of God.

As you read, you will realize that today the devil is still doing the same kind of thing he did throughout history. He will try to deceive you as he did Eve in the Garden of Eden. He will seek to destroy you as he did the little boy brought to Jesus in Matthew 17:14–15. His father said the devil threw the lad into the fire and into the water, but Jesus healed him. Satan will seek to disgrace you as he did the demoniac of Gadara, who left his home and friends, tore off his clothes, and lived in the cemetery. And he will try to damn you as he did Simon Magus, the sorcerer who tried to purchase the gift of God from Simon Peter. We must know these things about demon power and understand them before we can combat the devil and win.

Repression

Demon power is not spoken of in many religious circles today. Many people seem afraid of demons. Others simply don't believe in demons, so the subject is not mentioned. But I have noticed that the less we say about demons and the less we expose them, the more control they assume over human destiny. It is only when we pull the drapes back and expose demon power that we can set people free.

It is very interesting to me that God makes every human an expressionist. The moment a baby is born, the doctor spanks it. He wants expression. If he doesn't get it, he suspects the baby might be dead!

God desires exuberant expression from us. He wants our eyes to talk, our faces to light up. He made us to express something. Anyone who represses that function is doing the work of the devil.

It is a bad sign when a person becomes silent. A soul in solitude is headed for trouble. Eyes that gaze in a fixed stare reveal bondage of the soul. To lose the good spirit of joy and happiness is to take the road to a ruined personality. One who represses all his inner feelings becomes a walking dead man. The Bible commands us not to *"grieve the Holy Spirit"* (Eph. 4:30). I believe the word *"grieve"* could mean "do not repress" the Spirit.

To repress a person is to destroy the natural expression God gave him at birth. To repress a person is to check by power, to restrain from without. To repress a personality takes away the joy and gladness of that life. God did not create human lives to be restrained by an abnormal environment.

This second step toward demon possession is often found in churches and religions. Some people go to church and never experience the joy of salvation. Consider a man who goes to a worship service and takes with him a little boy or girl. They walk along the sidewalk chatting and laughing, but within fifty steps of the church something suddenly happens to the man. His eyes go into a fixed gaze and his body becomes rigid.

He walks softly into the church, finds his pew, and sits down. For the next hour he sits there like a mummy, expressionless. When the meeting is over he leaves. As he gets about fifty steps away from the church, he sighs and says, "I'm glad that's over for another week."

Much of religion today expresses nothing to the spirit of man. Instead, formal religion suppresses a person's fervent feelings toward God. In my services we often sing happy choruses because God's joy comes to us from expressing ourselves.

Many church members go to church as though it were a funeral parlor. If God did manifest Himself in any manner, it would scare them to death. According to the Bible, real worship is different. When the people dedicated Solomon's temple there was much expression—musical instruments and singing of praises to God. Many such illustrations can be seen throughout the Bible.

Sometimes repression begins at home. Every home should take a survey of its members. A child can be the repressor. When something goes wrong, he flies into a tantrum and it takes everyone in the home to get things normal again. Sometimes it can be a wife and mother who causes the family to tiptoe around. When something displeases her, she makes the home a miserable place for a week.

It can be a belligerent husband. The family may be happy and singing until he opens the door. Then he bellows and yells until everyone just dies inside. That man represses what could be a happy home.

Repression can happen at work. A foreman can be "as mean as the devil" to the men who work for him. He can curse and scream at the men until they are nervous wrecks. Eventually the men even hate to go to work. When they do go, they won't smile and will barely speak when the foreman is around. They become repressed.

You ask, "But what has this to do with the devil?" It is the devil who makes people act like this. Satan wants to steal all the joy and happiness from every human. We should be careful not to repress others, but rather let them express themselves under God.

Suppression

To suppress means to abnormally squeeze down, to crush, to conceal, as to suppress information.

Satan is very keen on suppression. It represents another step toward deterioration of emotions and the destruction of complete personal happiness.

Suppression comes from without. It is an unholy action because God and the entire Bible reveal dynamic expression with openness of desire and exuberance of feeling. When feelings are not expressed, they are suppressed or kept back. Let us realize that the devil causes suppression of the spiritual life.

Suppressed people are not energetic or enthusiastic about anything. A suppressed individual

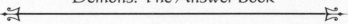

becomes listless and inactive—even disinterested in what goes on around him. If enough Christians were suppressed, Satan would have free rule in the world, with no one to oppose him and thwart his evil plans to control the world and its people.

Almost everyone has feelings of suppression at some time. The average person overcomes it after a few hours, or at most after a day or two. A word of comfort or encouragement from a friend, a passage from God's Word, a good night's rest, or a change of scenery is usually enough to bring new hope and renewed strength to begin living again. If suppression and melancholy hang on, however, the victim may be headed for serious trouble.

Depression

A man came into my office one day and said, "If you can't help me, I'm going to commit suicide."

He confessed that he hadn't kissed his wife in ten years. He would go for months without speaking to her. He would come home at night and read the newspaper while he ate. Then he would get up from the table, take his newspaper with him into his bedroom, lock the door, and retire. The next morning he would eat his breakfast, reading again, and then walk out of the house for work.

Looking at that man was like looking at death. I have never seen a man more depressed. There in my office I laid hands on him in the name of

Jesus and prayed a prayer of deliverance for him. Instantly the cloud left his mind. Joy came into his heart. He went home and became reconciled with his wife. He became a new creature. He began to work for Jesus.

The depression under which this man was living was humanly unbearable. He had decided it was better to be dead than alive, and he was ready to commit suicide. Christ broke the bondage of that depression and set him free.

It is sad to observe the great number of people in America today who are depressed. Depression is a broken spirit. A person is pressed down until his spirit is crushed. To remain depressed for a long period of time is of the devil and is not natural to life. God does not want anyone depressed and sad. Anyone who stays depressed for an extended time is sick. The devil takes advantage of those people and moves in with conflict and confusions that will destroy their happiness, their homes, their businesses, and maybe even their lives through suicide.

Traditions can contribute to depression. While I was holding meetings in a church in another city, I met a Christian woman who was still deeply depressed over the loss of her husband six months earlier. Her pastor told me her husband had been a fine Christian businessman and that she was a very capable businesswoman herself. She had no problem financially, but, following tradition, she had dressed

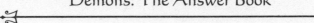

in black from head to toe. Every day for more than six months she had been in mourning. I could see she was carrying a burden of depression.

"Why are you wearing black?" I asked her.

"Oh," she said, "I'm in mourning for my dead husband."

"Was he a sinner?"

"Oh, no!" she exclaimed.

"Then why do you look so sad about his going to heaven?"

This was the first time anyone had spoken the truth to her about her melancholy. I asked her if she thought they wore black in heaven. She replied, "No, I think they wear white up there."

"Then why don't you dress cheerfully if your husband is in heaven where there is life? If he could see your downcast face and those mournful clothes, it would make him sad even in heaven."

Why did I talk to this lady so plainly? She was going downhill, fast becoming a recluse. She felt that if she smiled or laughed it would be disrespectful to her husband in heaven.

In the next service she came dressed in white from head to toe. She became one of the most inspiring Christians in the community. She now works in her church and leads a victorious Christian life. The devil was simply destroying her Christian witness with depression.

Tradition often demands a long face and a sad countenance, but the Bible says, *"A merry heart doeth good like a medicine"* (Prov. 17:22).

Many times depression is triggered by loss or serious trouble. Heavy financial burdens, family problems, or disappointments can depress a person, leaving him dejected and forlorn.

Depression is dangerous because it often brings about an abnormal state of inactivity. People may sit staring into space, hearing nothing, saying nothing, and doing nothing. Inside they feel a sadness too deep to express, too painful for tears. Their problems seem too desperate and complex to be solved. They have reached a point where they see no point to even trying any longer. They have lost hope. This is a big step toward complete satanic control of a person.

Are you depressed constantly? Then you need deliverance. And only Christ can deliver you. The cure for depression is to call upon Christ and place all your problems and heartaches and worries in His keeping. *"Casting all your care upon him; for he careth for you"* (1 Pet. 5:7). Be encouraged and say with the apostle Paul, *"I know whom I have believed, and am persuaded that he is able to keep that which I have committed unto him against that day"* (2 Tim. 1:12).

When the devil tries to weigh you down with sadness and perplexity, rebuke him in the name of

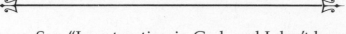

Jesus. Say, "I am trusting in God, and I don't have to be worried or anxious or sad or depressed. Go away, Satan, in Jesus' name!"

Some people are religiously depressed. They think there is great holiness in a long face. There is no biblical basis for this idea. God does not depress mankind; the devil is the depressor of human life.

By experience I have discovered that a downcast face and a sad soul won't help to resolve problems. It won't pay bills! It does no good at all.

In Psalm 103, King David said, *"Bless the Lord, O my soul: and all that is within me, bless his holy name"* (v. 1). That is the way you should get up every morning! Start the day blessing the Lord.

Oppression

The fifth stage through which the devil drags a person to destroy and possess him is what I call oppression.

To oppress someone is to weigh him down with something he is not able to carry. The children of Israel were oppressed in Egypt. They were treated cruelly, beaten unmercifully, and crushed down until they could carry their burdens no longer.

God the Father sent Jesus to this earth to heal all who were oppressed by the devil (Acts 10:38). This suggests that oppression can be in the realm of disease. Millions are oppressed in America. I do not believe disease is natural any more than a beautiful tree is natural with every kind of bug and disease covering its branches. I believe it is natural to be healthy and unnatural to be unhealthy. Disease is one of the devil's tools.

Millions of people are oppressed by fear. Some worry about going out of their minds. The devil wants them to think that. But God's Word says Satan is a liar and the father of lies. He wants to torment people. He wants to hurt them. And he wants to mock and laugh at God while he does it. But God's people do not have to suffer this terrible fear. One of the great blessings of Christianity is a strong mind that is capable of rejecting the unreasonable demands of fear.

A few years ago a woman came to me and said, "Brother Sumrall, my home is breaking to pieces. I can't stay in my house. When my husband leaves home to go to work in the morning, I just start shaking and I go to pieces. I have to run out the back door and go to my neighbor's. And I don't walk back into that house until my husband gets home.

"When he comes home from work, the dishes are just as they were when he left. I'm afraid to stay in my own house alone. What am I going to do?"

"Well," I said, "did you come to talk or to get help?"

"If you can help me," she answered, "then I want you to."

"Then you must do as I tell you after I have prayed. Tomorrow morning when your husband gets ready to go to work, go to the front door and kiss him goodbye. And since he usually closes the door, you say, 'Honey, I'm closing the door today.'

"Then you step back and close it just the way a fourteen-year-old would do it. [They know how to close doors. It seems like some of those doors may never open again!] After the door is shut, step back into the middle of the room and say, 'Devil, I'm staying in this house all day long. You get out of here. Jesus is here. In His name I command you to leave.' And when you say it, let the devil know you mean business. Then start singing. Sing our church songs all day long. When your husband comes home, he is going to be the most surprised man in town."

I was conducting a revival meeting, and the next night the woman came back. She was free. She said she had enjoyed a glorious day.

"I did exactly as you told me," she said. "I screamed out that I was going to stay in that house, looked around, and just cleaned and sang hymns all day long. It has been a wonderful day."

Two or three days later she assured me she still had no trouble.

The devil is an oppressor. God never intended for us to be slaves of oppression. We are His sons and daughters!

Satan may use many means to try to destroy you. He may try to crush your spirit through people you thought were your friends. He may seek to trample you down through disaster and woe. He may try to overpower you with a great display of demonic power that hurts you on all sides until you feel helpless against his cruel onslaught. He might weigh you down with an awesome sense of responsibility for all the people and actions in your family or community. He might even burden you with a feeling that all your trouble and misfortune is punishment from God for some great sin.

All these things fall into the category of demonic oppression. And oppression can be overcome. Exercise your Christian dominion over the devil's power. You do this by faith, prayer, and action. Ask God for faith to command His power in your life. Pray to strengthen your inner being. And act to overcome and destroy the works of the devil.

If the devil is oppressing you with disease, with fear, with nerve problems, with anything—receive deliverance now. Christ will set you free (John 8:36)!

Obsession

Jesus was obsessed with His own destiny— saving the world. The apostle Paul was obsessed with the Gospel of Jesus Christ so much that a Roman governor told him he was a madman. These were magnificent obsessions.

But there is also a negative obsession that destroys the human personality.

At this stage of demon domination, I doubt that the individual being hurt by Satan could be delivered without the assistance of another. I feel sure that a person who has regressed or is repressed can shake it off in Jesus' name and be free. I believe that a person who is suppressed or depressed, when reminded of the danger, can rid himself of it and have a joyful spirit. And it is possible for one who is oppressed to help himself.

But when we get to the sixth stage—obsession—then outside help is necessary. The reason for this is that obsession changes the mind. Black becomes white and white seems black. A straight thing is now crooked and a lie becomes the truth. This loss of perspective causes the person to be out of step with everybody else around him. He does not realize he is obsessed with some wicked thing.

What is obsession? By definition it is an "act of an evil spirit in besetting a person or impelling him to unreasonable action." The dictionary also says it is a persistent and inescapable preoccupation with an idea or emotion. This preoccupation usually has no relationship with reality.

I met a little lady in Chicago when I was speaking to a group of Christian businessmen there a few years ago. She weighed less than a hundred pounds, was poorly dressed, and her face registered deep apprehension. After the program she came up to me, looked around at the prosperous businessmen, and said, "All these people are against me."

I decided to go along with her. I looked up and asked, "They are? Which ones are against you?"

She pointed at the man who was in charge of the meeting. He was a very wealthy man, and probably did not even know the woman. She said, "I have to hide from these people who are against me," and with that she slipped out, going out of the building. It would have been useless for me to say, "No one wants to hurt you," for in her warped mind she was sure everyone was seeking her destruction.

Obsession can come by believing a lie. If what we believe is out of line with what others believe, we should check our beliefs and seek to know the truth. Otherwise, the devil may deceive us with an evil obsession.

Obsession can come through jealousy. A wife or husband may get an idea that their spouse is not loyal to them. This thing preys on the mind. The devil makes the idea take root and grow like a strong vine. Finally, every time the mate turns his back, the jealous one says, "Now he has done something wrong." Their very lives can be destroyed because of the evilness of jealousy.

I believe hatred can be an avenue to obsession. One can believe others dislike him and begin to hate them until he cannot think straight. He cannot see what is true because hatred has blinded him.

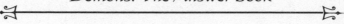
Certain sins can become an obsession. One may become overwhelmed by his immorality and be unable to see anything pure and holy because he is blinded with this obsession.

The devil has many avenues to invade the human psyche. When someone develops a complex in any form, that person should pray, read the Word of God, and consult a minister or a Christian friend whom they trust and can confide in.

An obsessed person eventually has no willpower. He has no strength to resist and he becomes a slave. His mind gets on one track and it is impossible to change his thinking.

Willpower is one of the great gifts God has given to us. We should never lend it to anybody through hypnotism, fortune-telling, drugs, alcohol, or anything else. Anything that can destroy your willpower should be avoided. God wants His children to be men and women who know right from wrong. They must let no obsession take over the mastery of their soul.

Once a person has fallen prey to demon obsession, he must draw close to Jesus Christ. He needs a man or woman of faith to pray a prayer of deliverance for him and ask God to set him free.

Possession

In this area extreme caution is necessary. The step from obsession to possession is a long one. The devil would like to push every obsessed person fully and finally into his clutches of full possession.

Up to this stage, a person is not truly demon-possessed. I do not find many people in this final state, although there are many in the other stages.

The demon-possessed person is under the absolute, total, complete jurisdiction of the devil. At this point he has no mind of his own. Satan is now the master of all that person's thinking and doing. He has full control of that life. The person has no spirit to reach out for God, no soul to pray for help! He is helpless in the hands of a diabolical monster.

There are many ways we can know when a person is demon-possessed.

I have observed in dealing with demon-possessed persons that often the devil uses the person's voice and throat to speak. I have heard men under the influence of demon power speak to me with the voice of a woman. I also have heard a woman speak with the gruff voice of a man.

Demon possession sometimes reveals itself in forms of insanity, both temporary and complete. Doctors who work in institutions and asylums know that a patient's mind may be very clear at one time and at another time the person becomes like an animal. This is the coming and going of demon power within the person. These people who are lost in a world of gloom, darkness, and misery have the saddest faces in the world. They have lost the power to rise above their problems. The devil has actually captured them and they live in his chains.

Often demon possession is easily observed in the eyes, for a person's personality frequently is projected through them. A demon-possessed person cannot look at others straight. He cannot hold up his head to you, for the devil will not let him.

The surest way to tell if one is demon-possessed is spiritual discernment. If God's Spirit is within me and the devil's spirit is within another person, when we meet there is a tremendous clash of spirits. It has nothing to do with personality; it is the warfare of opposing spirits.

Satan's power is as contagious as the measles. Those under his power want others under it too. A drug addict deceives others until they too are "hooked." Sexual perverts look for the unwary, to lead them into sin. Latent victims are urged into the trap by aggressors. People with fear and depression may have an unreasonable desire that others suffer as they do. So the first stages of demon possession often result from association with others already under the devil's control.

To some people the words "demon possession" mean something dirty or immoral. But we need to change our thinking about this subject. Some of the finest people in the world have been assaulted by the devil, and in some instances conquered. They need the help of Christ and the church right now. The Lord is just as willing to heal a person who is tormented by the devil as a person with a bad cold. Deliverance comes through the same kind of power, with the same anointing, and the same kind of faith. There is no difference whatsoever.

The Holy Spirit can resolve all problems. The church is commissioned to cast out devils. We must fulfill this commission.

I believe it is time for a great freedom action to be set in motion. Men and women of courage should set out to bring freedom to those who are regressed, repressed, suppressed, depressed, oppressed, obsessed, or even possessed by the devil's power. The same Christ who set the prisoners free two thousand years ago can set them free today.

8
Can a Christian Have a Demon?

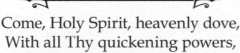

Come, Holy Spirit, heavenly dove,
With all Thy quickening powers,
Kindle a flame of sacred love,
In these cold hearts of ours.

—Isaac Watts,
"Come, Holy Spirit, Heavenly Dove"

The May 1978 issue of *The Tennessean* magazine carried a feature story about an east Nashville housewife who had evidently become possessed by a demon or was experiencing a vicious satanic attack. The woman, identified as Ann H., told the editors of *The Tennessean* her bizarre story, which had already made headlines in the Nashville papers.

According to Ann, a "lady" appeared in her bedroom one night. Ann had undergone surgery a few weeks earlier, and that particular evening she had taken antibiotics and dropped off into a sound sleep. Some time later she was awoken by the barking of dogs in the neighborhood. Then the thin bedroom curtains bloused out and a "lady" and two children appeared.

To Ann's horror, the "lady" moved to her bedside.

"I was praying, 'Lord, let me wake up!'" recalled Ann. But the figure moved closer. Ann described this spirit as having an almond-shaped face and pointed ears. Her mouth was similar to that of a rat, and her hair (under a cape) was pulled up on top of her head. Her eyes were "intense, like fire."

According to Ann, the "lady" beckoned for her to go with her, assuring her that her worries and suffering were over. (Ann's husband, a building contractor, had not been able to find steady work; Ann herself had not been well.) As the "lady" moved still closer, Ann heard a voice say, "You and your damned God. You don't need God. You're with me." As this figure bent over her bed, Ann was gripped with fear, but suddenly she was enveloped by a peace she had never before experienced.

This was the first of numerous encounters this housewife claims to have had with the "lady." The children who first appeared with her never reappeared, and as far as I know, Ann does not know the identity of either the "lady" or the children.

Ann told reporters that the encounter may have been brought on by what had happened to her a few weeks earlier when she shared a room with an elderly woman in Nashville's General Hospital. The woman seemed to notice Ann, but did not say anything for the first two days. Then, Ann says, "She turned toward me, and began to move her lips. No sound came out....I told her I'd try to call the nurses, and I did. And then the woman said, very distinctly, 'You're doomed to hell.' Just as she said that, her eyes locked on me and she died."

The "lady" has developed a jealousy about Ann's husband and children, reported *The Tennessean*. "She has a temper and when she's mad she sometimes touches me violently. It feels like dry ice...and she always wants to take my breath; she seems to need it," Ann says.

One winter night Ann was awakened and told, evidently by the "lady," to turn off the gas logs in the living room and then turn on the gas. She obeyed. Had not her husband awakened and smelled the fumes, the entire family might have perished.

Once, Ann stopped breathing and felt she had "physically died," and remembers "looking back on my body lying in bed and my husband and two of

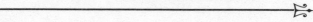

my children trying to revive me." Ann felt "warm and secure" wrapped in the lady's cape, but on seeing her husband and children crying, she knew she had to return to them.

Following several attempts to remove the "lady" (who has physically abused her), Ann now says, "I've gotten to where I just accept her. I know she'll be with me as long as I live."

The magazine says that Ann is a Southern Baptist, and that more than once pastors and "groups of people of various denominations" have prayed with her, but to no avail.

No doubt this case of an apparently Christian woman has stirred thoughtful interest among people in Nashville. The magazine judged interest so keen that it followed with another story in July. Seventeen prominent ministers and psychiatrists (including two hypnotists) were asked if they thought it "possible for a person to be possessed by a demon." None of the clinicians answered a definite yes, although some gave a qualified yes. Replies from pastors and rabbis ranged from two who said no to seven who responded with a definite yes.

One pastor answered as I would have many years ago. He said he did not believe a Christian can be possessed. "They can be oppressed and they can be under attack," he said, "but you cannot be possessed by Jesus Christ and by a demon...."

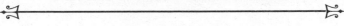

Definitions

Can a Christian be demon-possessed? It becomes a matter of definitions when you really study the question carefully. What is a Christian? When you start dealing with definitions, you are dealing with problems, because there are too many definitions.

A person may belong to First Church and think he cannot be demon-possessed. That has nothing to do with the problem at all. If he is hurt, he needs help. You reach people when you deal with them in relation to their needs rather than their tags.

The Bible teaches very strongly the security of the believer. No devil ever wanted to get inside Paul. They wanted to run from him as far as they could. And nowhere does the Bible tell anyone to be afraid of the devil. *"Resist the devil, and he will flee from you"* (James 4:7). We have a right to make him run. But when we start playing in his territory, we are in danger.

Leave the Devil's Territory Alone!

Not long ago, on a Sunday night in our church, several people came forward for prayer at the close of the service. Among them was a Sunday school teacher. When it came time for me to pray for her, I had no freedom to pray. Something was wrong. Finally I asked what the matter was and to my surprise a man's voice answered out of her mouth.

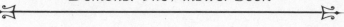

"She came to see the movie in the adult theater and I entered her," the spirit said. "I had every right to her."

When I asked the woman if this were true, she admitted it. She said she had felt that she needed to know what went on in the movie houses that show X-rated films in order to teach against it.

"No you didn't," I said. "You went in there and enjoyed what you saw." She nodded her head.

I believe that when she stepped into the theater she entered Satan's territory and opened herself to a demon. Knowing this, I laid my hands upon her and commanded the evil spirit to leave. It obeyed.

This opened an avenue of thinking to me. I began to understand that when a Christian goes into the devil's territory, unless intending to do battle and rescue lost souls, that Christian becomes vulnerable to whatever Satan offers, even to being invaded by an evil spirit.

While Louise and I lived in Hong Kong we never feared Communist China. From our apartment we could see the harbor where the American Seventh Fleet had its aircraft carriers, destroyers, and many submarines. When we would go about the city, at certain places we could see large numbers of crack British troops and large guns. We felt secure as long as we stayed within the borders of Hong Kong.

At one place there was a sign posted by a bridge, which said, "Communist China ahead of you. Do not advance further unless you have credentials to do so." If I had ventured to the border and entered Red China, I would have cancelled my right to protection by American and British forces. The same is true of Christian living. When you play with sin you cannot cancel your salvation, but you can forfeit the covering of the blood to keep Satan from doing as he pleases.

I am personally convinced that anger can be a spirit and that if a Christian allows himself or herself to vent anger without restraint, there is a very real danger of the entrance of a spirit of anger.

I am convinced that adultery is a spirit. A prominent pastor told me that for more than a year he was within the grips of a spirit of adultery. It was so strong that cold perspiration would run off his fingertips until he yielded to his forbidden desires. Only a prayer of deliverance finally set him free.

Professing church members can open themselves to a spirit of jealousy. Some women have a jealous spirit. They can have the best husband in the world and still accuse him whenever he walks in the door. The only explanation is a spirit of jealousy.

There is such a thing as a spirit of blasphemy. It is evident everywhere today, and Christians need to be on their guard. Foul language and cursing has gushed up from the gutters and back alleys; it has entered our living rooms and become commonplace in the media. Some people cannot speak a sentence without blaspheming the name of God. These evil spirits must be cast out before people can be free.

Ananias and Sapphira were a part of the first church in Jerusalem. When they saw how Barnabas received such acclaim for donating his property, they decided to sell theirs. But they could not bring themselves to give away all of the money. They brought part of it to the apostles and pretended it was the full amount. The Holy Spirit showed Peter it was a lie. (See Acts 5:1–11.) Both Ananias and Sapphira were struck dead for their lies.

A lying spirit haunts God's children today. It is a terribly deceptive spirit, and many children of God need to be set free from its curse.

In summary, I am of the opinion that evil spirits can invade and enter the life of a believer. Paul warned that

> *The servant of the Lord must not strive; but be gentle unto all men...in meekness instructing those that oppose themselves; if God peradventure will give them repentance to the acknowledging of the truth; and that they **may recover themselves out of the snare of the devil, who are taken captive by him at his will.***
>
> (2 Tim. 2:24–26, emphasis added)

If we obey the command to *"be filled with the Spirit"* (Eph. 5:18), then we give no place to the devil in our lives.

9
Satan's Subtle Snares

Regard not them that have familiar spirits,
neither seek after wizards, to be defiled by them:
I am the LORD your God.

—Leviticus 19:31

The devil advertises his services to today's society in dozens of ways. Never out in the open, he nevertheless is not far from the surface. In the newspapers he charms millions with the so-called guidance of the ages, written in the daily horoscopes. Bookracks at the supermarkets and newsstands hawk his wares, inviting the reader to read books with themes of exorcism, witchcraft, and the like. Movie theaters do his bidding, enticing the vulnerable young and old alike to explore the world of the unknown, the weird, and the devilish. Television joins the trend by highlighting Satan worship in a cops-and-robbers evening show. The mail dispenses the devil's products, offering a full set of encyclopedia on the supernatural or the latest slick porno magazine.

Is It Really Harmless?

An unsuspecting tourist brings home a souvenir amulet or idol from another country and places it innocently in the living room, never thinking that by doing so he may be playing with the devil. Much of Satan's activity dazzles the senses. It seems so harmless. But is it?

When one of our three sons was thirteen, he and his friends became enamored with the Beatles' music for a time. Word got around high school that there was a secret message on one of their records if it were played backward, so the boys tried it. All Sunday afternoon they tried to decipher a message.

My wife and I were sitting downstairs that evening as my son rushed into the room, frightened, and cried, "Dad, the devil's in my room!"

I didn't know what to make of it. "Well, if he's there, then you're going to have to tell me how he got there," I said.

He told me what he and his friends had been doing. I could see that he was in no shape to return to the room, so I prayed with him and told him he would sleep with his mother and I would go upstairs to his room.

When I reached the room, I knew a devil was there. The feeling was strange. It made my flesh crawl. But I had dealt with the devil before and so I wasted no time in taking charge. Slamming the door, I said, "You wicked devil, what right do you have coming into my house! This house is cleansed by the blood of Jesus Christ. I want you to know I've already claimed the covering of Jesus' blood for my son, and now I'm ordering you to get out of this house and never return. Furthermore, I'm sleeping in this room and I will not be bothered by you. I'm not afraid of you; now get out, in the name of Jesus."

I slept in my son's room that night, and the devil never bothered us again.

A few years ago, three girls from our church in South Bend were attending Bible school in the Midwest when they received a terrible scare. For fun, they had begun fooling around with a Ouija board. In the evening they would sit around, place their fingers on the board, and ask, "Who is my boyfriend?" or "What will I do when I get out of school?"

This went on for several weeks until one night one of the girls asked, "Who are you? Who is giving us these answers to our questions?" The answer came: "I am Satan."

This so terrified one of the girls that she called home and her mother called me to ask for prayer.

The girls never dreamed they were making contact with the evil supernatural world.

Shortly after his conversion, Arlindo Barbosa de Oliviera of Brazil came to America at the invitation of our church and told his personal story. You may remember from earlier chapters that he had been a witch doctor for forty years and had been baptized to the devil. As a member of the large spiritist cult in Brazil, he said he had heard the voice of the devil hundreds of times while in a trance and had drunk flaming rum and eaten ground glass. After serving the devil all those years, he says Jesus Christ appeared to him and he was saved.

We recorded Arlindo's story and produced the "Witch Doctor" record. One of our youths, who was attending a Christian university, owned a copy of this record. One night in his dormitory room he played it for two of his friends. The two boys began to mock and laugh at what they were hearing. But while the record was playing, they went berserk. Afterward, both of them had to receive psychiatric care before resuming their studies. The boy who had played the record got on a train and came home, and his mother called me to pray for him. He was badly shaken by the incident.

It had seemed such an innocent thing to mock the devil's voice on a recording, but the devil is not to be taken lightly.

America's climate today makes such "harmless" activities as these fairly commonplace. The influence of godliness and righteousness in our nation has waned; most people are spiritually starved, although forty-three percent attend church with some degree of regularity. This moral bankruptcy fosters the ideal environment for the occult and superstitions.

Forbidden Territory

African slaves with their voodoo brought much superstition and fear with them in the early days of America. The native Indian's life has always been heavily burdened by witchcraft, evil spirits, and magic. From England, America inherited ghost stories that abound in superstition. And today people by the thousands are turning back to these things rather than to the living God.

The Bible is very clear about the occult. It is forbidden. In Leviticus 19:31, Moses commanded the Israelites not to regard those who have familiar spirits or seek after wizards. *"I am the LORD your God,"* God said. It was not the Lord's will for His people to turn to a negative, lying, demonic source. He was available for them and their future was in His hands.

Superstition Analyzed

The dictionary defines superstition as "an irrational attitude of mind toward the supernatural, nature, or God, proceeding from ignorance, unreasoning fear of the unknown or the mysterious; a

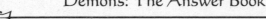
belief in magic or chance, or the like." Our English word is taken from the Latin *superstitio*, which means "a standing over or above, as in wonder or awe." Superstitions are traditions, old tales, and theories still lacking proven truth.

Superstition has to do with charms, spells, good and evil spirits, foretelling of events, unusual forces, and powers operating in objects and beings. They often reveal strange and seemingly inexplicable powers and energies that, as we will see, find their beginnings in ignorance, selfishness, greed, and cultish worship.

It is a remarkable paradox that although we live in history's most scientific age, there is more superstition today than ever. Millions are probing astrology, occult faiths, Indian mysticism, and all kinds of strange and seemingly mystic powers. There is actually an army of fortune-tellers, clairvoyants, palmists, crystal-ball gazers, astrologers, and gurus marching across the stage of the modern world, begging to be heard and exhibiting their strange wares.

Man can reach supernatural elements through the ability of demonic power. In giving one's life over to the devil, one has the possibility of reaching into the realm of demonic power. Superstition could open the mind's door to believe the lies of Satan. Error often begins with ignorance. One who is ignorant of God and begins seeking hidden realities without God or without the Bible may end up with the devil leading him around as if he had a hook in his nose.

The Age-Old Enemies

Divine faith and superstition are age-old enemies. Faith is the living, dynamic relationship between man and his resurrected Savior, while superstition is the willful desire of unregenerate man to rule the invisible world without a divine Savior. The sinner seeking the supernatural has one purpose in mind: to control mystic powers for self-gratification, not glorification of the Lord. In superstition there is no spiritual life, there are no morals, and there is no character.

Superstition was born because man in his deepest being longs for the supernatural. God made him this way so he would seek after heaven. The spirit and soul of man disdains the material way of life.

Superstition and Fear

Ministering in a large number of countries of the world for more than forty years, I have come to know the deep fears in the hearts of the heathen. They are afraid of God and of demons. They are afraid of the spirits of the dead and departed. They live in mortal fear of the unknown and of the future. They are tortured by a multitude of superstitions handed down to them from generation to generation.

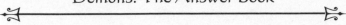

All superstition is motivated by fear. The traditions and legends surrounding Friday the thirteenth are good examples. The word "Friday" comes from the German goddess Freya, who was supposed to be the goddess of love, matrimony, and the home. The horse was the goddess Freya's sacred animal. It was sacrificed and eaten on her feast day and at special celebrations such as weddings. Because of this the early church, especially the Roman Catholic Church, would not allow meat to be eaten on Friday. From this superstition, Friday the thirteenth became known as an unlucky day. The number itself took on many superstitions. I have sat at a table with influential people when there were thirteen at the table, and one was asked to leave and sit by himself!

Superstitious fears can ruin a person's health. A businessman I know of went to a doctor because he was nervous, frustrated, and on the verge of mental collapse. The doctor could find nothing wrong physically, but he did discover that the businessman was an ardent believer in astrology. He had come to believe that because of the opposition of the planets Mars and Saturn and the unfavorable position of the moon, his condition was incurable. Nothing the doctor could say would sway the man's opinion, and I do not know if he was ever cured.

The devil loves to destroy a life through superstition. Multitudes in this country follow the phantoms in the sky out of fear, rather than letting their loving Creator guide and direct their lives.

Hypnotism

There is a strong hint of hypnotism even in the earliest days of earth's existence. In the Garden of Eden, is it not possible that the serpent hypnotized Eve, even as a snake petrifies a rabbit with its piercing gaze and magnetic rhythm? Lucifer, master of all fallen wisdom, whispered the illegal suggestion to Mother Eve. Gripping her mind through his devilish eyes, did he induce the state of unconcern that made her forget God's command? We know that he lied to her. "You will be like gods, and God doesn't want you to be like him. So He's holding information back from you!" And Eve, paying heed to the seducer's voice, did what he suggested. Sin entered the human race. (See Genesis 3:1–6.)

A hypnotized person is in a state of abnormal concentration induced by an operator—a description that could be used with equal accuracy to explain the condition of a demon-possessed person. Medical doctors know that hypnosis brings a change in a person's conscious awareness. The consciousness narrows, much as it does during a dream or a vision. But the hypnotized person is different from a sleeping person. He or she can walk, talk, write, or remain quiet. In most cases he will obey suggestions given him by the hypnotist.

It has been said that no subject can be induced to do anything contrary to his own moral principles. Scientists have proven, however, that hypnotized

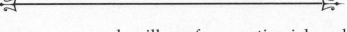

persons can and will perform antisocial and even self-destructive acts under deception by the operator.

A normally modest woman, for example, would refuse point-blank to remove her clothing under hypnosis if the suggestion were made directly. But if the operator suggested she was in the seclusion of her own bathroom, she might well disrobe before an audience of people. The subject, then, is at the mercy of the operator to a considerable degree—much more than anyone should be!

The Lord Jesus, speaking of the end of this age, warned His disciples, *"Take heed that no man deceive you"* (Matt. 24:4). Hypnosis is a form of deception. It has no divine life that can make a man better or cleaner or happier. All it can do is open the soul's door to possible demon invasion. Your mind must not be clouded by fear and phobia. It must not be confused by conflicting ideas. It must not be yielded to strange, psychic powers. At all costs, your mind must not be destroyed because it is the seat of your will. With your mind you must make all the proper decisions about how to live and prepare yourself to meet with God at the coming of our Lord Jesus Christ.

I prophesy that in the days ahead, before Jesus Christ returns, millions in America will have turned to every kind of spiritism, including hypnotism. Man will be offered religion that soothes the conscience, seemingly smoothes the rugged path of sin, and leads into sweet forgetfulness and eternal reincarnating bliss—bliss without the blood of Jesus and ecstasy without eternal life.

I urge Christians, indeed all people, not to offer their minds to anyone who wishes to hypnotize them and never to attend a meeting of oriental cults, which are demon-inspired. Rather, I urge you to keep yourselves clean and pure before God, and to walk in His ways and to serve Him.

I challenge you to have the mind of Christ: a strong mind, a dedicated mind. In Genesis 1:26–27 it is recorded that God created man to have dominion on earth. This dominion is achieved through your mind.

With Christ in your heart you do not need other guidance. He will guide you to a joyful tomorrow. The Bible declares that our Christian life is to be a walk of faith, but God has promised to be with us every step of the way. In these last days, may the Lord Jesus Christ keep you— your mind, spirit, soul, and body—by His mighty power.

> *Finally, brethren, whatsoever things are true, whatsoever things are honest, whatsoever things are just, whatsoever things are pure, whatsoever things are lovely, whatsoever things are of good report; if there be any virtue, and if there be any praise, **think on these things**.*
>
> (Phil. 4:8, emphasis added)

Destroying Emblems of Demon Power

God warns His people against all supernaturalism that is not of Him. In the first century, Paul warned against idols that are symbols of evil supernaturalism.

> *What say I then? that the idol is any thing, or that which is offered in sacrifice to idols is any thing? But I say, that the things which the Gentiles sacrifice, they sacrifice to devils, and not to God: and I would not that ye should have fellowship with devils.* (1 Cor. 10:19–20)

God has His symbols of power. In the Old Testament, the ark of God symbolized His presence and His holiness. When the Philistines captured the ark of God they placed it inside their temple, beside their god Dagon. The next morning Dagon lay broken on the ground at the foot of the ark. The presence of God in the symbolic ark destroyed Dagon. (See 1 Samuel 5:1–4.)

The devil has symbols of power also. Perhaps the most easily recognized symbols are the idols made of clay, stone, wood, or iron. These idols have been brought to America and sold. Unsuspecting tourists have brought them back from Asia and other parts of the world, not knowing that there is evil attached to these symbols of power in the devil's realm.

A teacher in a British Bible school told me that each morning his students became drowsy and some fell asleep while he was teaching. At first, he said, he thought the students were having too much for breakfast—but no one gets too much breakfast in Bible school!

He began looking around the classroom; on a window ledge he discovered a bronze serpent from India—a coiled cobra, worshipped in India as a god. Without telling anyone that he was doing so, he removed the idol from the room. No one became drowsy the next morning or thereafter.

In China I visited a large Buddhist temple where the priests showed me their gods, many of which were ugly, frightening idols with eight or ten arms. Pointing to one about sixteen feet high I asked the priest, "How can that idol help you?"

He was very polite. "You don't understand, being a foreigner," he replied. "That idol does not have power. We all know that. The spirit of that idol is elsewhere right now, but if I were to bring incense and food and place it before that idol and start praying, something would start happening."

Then he took me to the rear of the idol and pointed to a hole. "That is where the spirit goes in and out," he said. "It wants worship. If I come and kneel here and offer an offering and burn incense or candles, immediately the spirit comes and communicates with me."

The idol was a symbol for the demon spirit. The grotesque face of that idol was something the artist designed under the power of the devil. A Christian should have no such idols in his home, office, work-place—anywhere.

While I was pastoring in Manila, we helped build a tribal church in the headhunter country of Luzon in the Philippines. While preaching there they showed me a tree where spirits live. It is a symbol of demon power. It did not have a leaf on it and was greasy in appearance, probably because the worshippers had wiped their hands on it. The boughs were gnarled and crooked. The tribe said their spirit gods lived in the tree and that they offered incense and offerings at the foot of it.

Even the cross can be a symbol of Satan's power. When praying for Clarita Villanueva in the Bilibid prison, I noticed she wore a strange metal cross around her neck. Once she climbed under the desk of the chief of police and complained that she had lost her cross. The chief kicked her and said, "Come out from there; I don't know anything about your cross."

To prove that he did not know anything, he turned both of his front pockets wrong side out and shook them. Then he put his pockets back and Clarita said, "Look again." The policeman plunged his hand into his pocket and found her metal cross. It frightened him, and four days later he died.

The crystal ball is another device of Satan's power. With such a ball Jeanne Dixon and others who claim clairvoyance make predictions. They also use a deck of cards for fortune-telling. When a person touches that deck of cards, they tell his fortune. Many Christian households have some professional playing cards. Almost every witch doctor and fortune-teller in the world uses these to help them in their business. They have no place in the home of a Christian.

Is there any biblical basis for destroying the symbols of demon power? In the early church at Ephesus, the power of God became so strong that Luke wrote,

> *And many that believed came, and confessed, and showed their deeds. Many of them also which used curious arts brought their books together, and burned them before all men: and they counted the price of them, and found it fifty thousand pieces of silver. So mightily grew the word of God and prevailed.* (Acts 19:18–20)

This was a great fortune. At that time, thirty pieces of silver was the price of a slave. This means that with fifty thousand pieces of silver they could have bought 1,666 slaves!

If the early Christians were careful to clean out every symbol of the devil's power around them, you and I must do the same. We must clean out our hearts, what we wear on our bodies, and our homes. We must dig out the very roots of superstition and all that has to do with the devil's power. Believers must place their lives in the hand of God

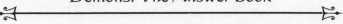

to guide them every day. We don't have to know what is going to happen tomorrow. If we did, we would not need to walk by faith. Unwarranted curiosity about the mysterious unknown may lead the believer into one of Satan's subtle snares.

10
Taking Authority
over Demons

And though the fiends on every hand
Were threatening to devour us
We would not waver from our stand
They cannot overpower us.
This world's prince may rave,
However he behave, he can do no ill.
God's truth abideth still.
One little word shall fell him.

—Martin Luther,
"A Mighty Fortress Is Our God"

During the time when *The Exorcist* was popular, I received a call from the David Susskind television show in New York, asking me to appear on his program. When I wanted to know why they were inviting me, they said they had read a booklet I had written and that they wished to bill me as an exorcist. I agreed to go on one condition—that I not be singled out as some phenomenon. I told them there is nothing peculiar about an exorcist and that every Christian could be one. I said I had never gone about looking for devils in order to cast them out. They must have changed their minds and decided they didn't want me after all. Apparently I wasn't peculiar enough.

Every Christian's Right

I meant what I told them. I have had forty years' experience in taking authority over demon power, but I do not consider myself unique. Dominion over Satan is every Christian's right by the blood of Jesus Christ.

A Christian who exercises dominion knows how to appropriate the fullness of God's provision for discipleship. He lives a victorious life above and beyond fear and phobias, superstition and evil curses. He is radiant and forceful in Christ.

Dominion Defined

Dominion extends to the believer much like links in a chain. It begins with God the Father who is supreme, all-powerful, all-wise, and present everywhere, the Creator of all things. God possesses infinite dominion.

The chain of dominion moves to the Lord Jesus Christ in whom dwells *"all the fulness of the*

Godhead bodily" (Col. 2:9). Jesus exhibited dominion in every stage of His life. His virgin birth transcended the known laws of nature. (See Luke 1:31–35.) He further demonstrated dominion over nature by turning water into wine, walking on water, multiplying bread and fish to feed more than five thousand hungry people, and calming the tempestuous sea. Jesus showed His dominion over sickness and disease by never failing to heal those brought to Him. (See Matthew 8:16.) He even asserted dominion over the grave by rising from the dead. (See Luke 24:6.)

Throughout His life, Jesus demonstrated His supreme dominion over devils. Even though they would rage against their victims, making a final effort to keep them in bondage, every one of them yielded to the Lord's command and begged for mercy as Jesus cast them out.

No man ever lived and taught dominion as Jesus did. The Bible says that in Him *"are hid all the treasures of wisdom and knowledge"* (Col. 2:3). He concluded His earthly ministry by declaring, *"All power is given unto me in heaven and in earth"* (Matt. 28:18). This is supreme dominion.

Great dominion resides in the blood of Jesus. He came to this world to shed His blood as a sacrifice for man's sin. The Bible says, *"The life of the flesh is in the blood"* (Lev. 17:11); therefore, Christ's blood had to be shed. Jesus said to His disciples, *"This is my blood...which is shed for many for the remission of sins"* (Matt. 26:28). The holy, saving blood of Jesus Christ has power and dominion.

There is no divine forgiveness outside the shed blood of Jesus Christ.

But if we walk in the light, as he is in the light, we have fellowship one with another, and the blood of Jesus Christ his Son cleanseth us from all sin.

(1 John 1:7)

Peter wrote,

Forasmuch as ye know that ye were not redeemed with corruptible things, as silver and gold, from your vain conversation received by tradition [handed down] *from your fathers; but with the precious blood of Christ.* (1 Pet. 1:18–19)

Paul declared dominion in Christ's blood also.

And, having made peace through the blood of his cross, by him to reconcile all things unto himself.
(Col. 1:20; see also Rev. 1:5; 5:9, 12:11.)

There is also remarkable dominion in the Bible. It is the only living Book known to man, possessing great power to preserve itself and to bless all humanity. The Bible is God's inspired Word. I believe with the writer of Hebrews:

For the word of God is quick [living and active], *and powerful, and sharper than any twoedged sword, piercing even to the dividing asunder of soul and spirit, and of the joints and marrow, and is a*

discerner of the thoughts and intents of the heart.
(Heb. 4:12)

Since the Bible is the Word of God, it has unique authority over all other books. God has invested dominion in His written Word.

Jesus said of His prophetic Word, *"One jot or one tittle shall in no wise pass from the law, till all be fulfilled"* (Matt. 5:18). The eternalness of the Word is demonstrated when Christ said, *"Heaven and earth shall pass away, but my words shall not pass away"* (Matt. 24:35).

God spoke worlds into existence by His Word (Heb. 11:3). Peter and James declared we are spiritually born by the Word of God (1 Pet. 1:23; James 1:18). God's Word makes a believer a partaker of His nature (2 Pet. 1:4). Faith comes through hearing God's Word (Rom. 10:17), effects cleansing (Eph. 5:25–26), and gives assurance of everlasting life (1 John 5:13). When Christ answered Satan during the great temptations, He declared, *"It is written.... It is written....It is written...."* (See Matthew 4:4–10.) In this way He defeated the devil. There is great dominion in the Word.

The Holy Spirit is also an important link in the chain through which dominion extends to the believer. He has the power to do great miracles. He moves and no one can hinder Him. The Holy Spirit, as the third person of the triune God, knows no limit in time, energy, or space. He is the Comforter

(John 14:16, 26); He guides the believer (Rom. 8:14); He convicts the sinner (John 16:8); He is the Spirit of truth (John 16:13).

Through the divine operation of the Spirit, a disciple can possess dominion and be the final link in the chain. The Lord Jesus Christ perpetuated dominion on earth by giving power to His disciples. *"Behold, I give unto you power to tread on serpents and scorpions, and over all the power of the enemy: and nothing shall by any means hurt you"* (Luke 10:19).

Church leaders in every age have recognized the evil presence of man's great foe, the devil, and have exerted dominion over him. In the fourth century, Augustine wrote:

> What spirit can that be which by a hidden inspiration stirs men's corruption, and goads them into adultery, and feeds on the fullfledged iniquity, unless it be the same that finds pleasure in such religious ceremonies, sets in the temples images of devils, and loves to see in play the images of vices; that whispers in secret some righteous sayings to deceive the few who are good, and scatters in public invitations to profligacy, to gain possession of the millions who are wicked? [1]

Thomas Aquinas (1225–1274) assumed the reality of demons, spoke of exorcisms, and had no doubt that their power was greater than that of man, although not as great as God's.

Many popes wrote letters dealing with the devil and witchcraft. John Calvin frequently referred his readers to Ephesians 6:11–12, which starkly sums up the human battle with evil spirits.

No Christian of earlier times, perhaps, surpassed Martin Luther in the serious manner in which he perceived the devil's attacks upon himself. Historian Roland Bainton quotes one method Luther used in taking authority over Satan:

> When I go to bed, the devil is always waiting for me. When he begins to plague me, I give him this answer: "Devil, I must sleep. That's God's command, 'Work by day, sleep by night.' So go away." If that doesn't work and he brings out a catalog of sins, I say, "Yes, old fellow, I know all about it. And I know some more you have overlooked. Here are a few extra. Put them down." If he still won't quit and presses me hard and accuses me as a sinner, I scorn him. [2]

In the same context, Bainton points out that Luther did not necessarily follow his own advice. "Don't argue with the devil," he would say. "He has had five thousand years of experience. He has tried out all his tricks on Adam, Abraham, and David, and he knows exactly the weak spots." All the more reason to know how to take dominion!

Dominion Is for You

Who may exercise authority over demons? Is the victorious life only for a chosen few, for Paul and Luther, for Amy Carmichael and Corrie ten Boom, for pastors and missionaries? I believe the promises of the New Testament are always to any and every true disciple. Christ said,

> *Behold, I give unto you power to tread on serpents and scorpions, and over all the power of the enemy: and nothing shall by any means hurt you.* (Luke 10:19)

Dominion is for you if you are seeking to be a disciple of Jesus.

After a person is converted, the devil attempts in every way to continue deceiving him. He promotes the idea that Satan is not real. Failing that, he tries to keep the new Christian from knowing there is dominion over the devil. Satan knows that when the believer is aware of his privileges and power, he (Satan) will be completely defeated and his works destroyed.

An age-old strategy of the devil is to attack the believer in the area of how he represents himself or his "confession." He knows a person will never rise above the quality of his faith. Instead of making the promises of God what he lives by, a believer may only bemoan his sickness and faults and weakness. Therefore, if you do not claim the promised power of God in your life, the devil can keep you in bondage.

People do not like substitutes. For this reason an automobile dealer will display a sign over his business that reads "Authorized Dealer." The sign means a consumer can expect genuine parts for his car and factory-trained mechanics to install them. In the spiritual realm, Bible-believing Christians are God's authorized dealers of His dominion. They have what God wants this world to have. It would be most fitting, therefore, for the church to put out a sign saying, "Authorized Dealer of God's Spirit and Power."

The early church had this dominion. Before He ascended to heaven, Jesus Christ said, *"Ye shall receive power, after that the Holy Ghost is come upon you"* (Acts 1:8). The world has known of that power.

That this dominion was to continue after Pentecost is evident. Peter said,

> *For the promise is unto you, and to your children, and to all that are afar off, even as many as the Lord our God shall call.* (Acts 2:39)

The New Testament emphasizes that this divine dominion was not exclusively for the apostles. (See Acts 6:8; 8:5–8.) I have always encouraged church members to pray not only for themselves, but also for others who are sick or in need—and to expect miracles from God. Quite often these laypeople report dramatic answers to their prayers. Clearly, dominion is not for a select few; it is for every disciple of the Lord Jesus.

Boundaries of Dominion

Only Christ Himself can set the boundaries or categories of the dominion of His disciples. The *"keys of the kingdom of heaven"* (Matt. 16:19), which He delivered to Peter, show us what these boundaries are.

First, on the day of Pentecost, Peter used a key of the kingdom by preaching the great prophetic message that inaugurated the New Testament church. Second, at the Beautiful Gate of the Jerusalem temple, Peter used another key. The lame man who had never walked was instantly healed. This miracle opened the door of the kingdom for healing during the dispensation of grace. What a thrilling key! Third, on the housetop of Simon the tanner, Peter received the revelation of world revival and global participation in salvation. With his revelation key he freed the prisoners of the nations. These keys of the kingdom have forever been and still are in the church of Jesus Christ.

In Mark 16:16, Jesus said, *"He that believeth and is baptized shall be saved."* This is the key every Gospel preacher can hold. But in the same verse He also said, *"He that believeth not shall be damned."* This is the ministry of binding and loosing. Whatever is bound on earth will be bound in heaven, Jesus said; and whatever is loosed on earth will be loosed in heaven (Matt. 16:19). Christ recognizes the believer's authority to preach the Gospel, and when sinners make their decision either for salvation or against Christ, heaven accepts the verdict.

Spiritual dominion is not exclusively a communal or collective power, it is for the individual as well. Many times a person must fight and conquer alone. The tendency today is to identify with large groups. People wish to be associated with big organizations. In much of modern warfare soldiers may never see the enemy at all; their guns and rockets and bombs are long-range. But the spiritual battle is for the individual. To win this battle you must personally have dominion from Christ. If we can see that our personal conflict must be a personal victory, we are a long way toward dominion.

Dominion over Sin

We don't have to be slaves to sin. We don't have to yield to temptation. Paul declared, *"For sin shall not have dominion over you"* (Rom. 6:14). David prayed, *"Order my steps in thy word: and let not any iniquity have dominion over me"* (Ps. 119:133). When our steps are ordered by Jesus, and when His Word is a part of our very beings, we are invested with might and authority.

Dominion over Thought Life

Our minds should not be garbage containers. We cannot avoid temptation and enticement, but we do not have to give in. A well-known saying goes, "You can't keep the birds from flying over your head, but you can keep them from building a nest in your hair." Every disciple can and must assert dominion, bringing every wild and unspiritual thought into captivity. (See 2 Corinthians 10:4–5.)

Dominion over Disease

Sickness can be made obedient to the Word of power and authority. In the Great Commission Jesus said, *"These signs shall follow them that believe…. They shall lay hands on the sick, and they shall recover"* (Mark 16:17–18).

Centuries earlier, Moses said sickness is a curse (Deut. 28:59–61). All curses lose their power over a child of God. *"Christ hath redeemed us from the curse of the law, being made a curse for us"* (Gal. 3:13). We are *"bought with a price"* and therefore we are to glorify God in our bodies and our spirits, *"which are God's"* (1 Cor. 6:20). It glorifies God for you to have dominion in your spirit and in your body.

The devil has power, as he did with Job, to bring disease upon you. But as a Christian you possess divine authorization to rebuke, renounce, and destroy all the authority of the devil. You must exercise your rights. If necessary, quote the source of your power. Just as a policeman says, "In the name of the law, stop," you as Christ's disciple must say, "In Jesus' name, I am healed."

God promised that none of the diseases of Eygpt would come upon the Israelites. Jesus came into the world to destroy the works of the devil. Christians who are not grounded in the Word are not aware of their dominion in this strategic area. They do not know they have authority to resist the devil and works of Lucifer. I find that the devil is an expert in fifth-column tactics. He sneaks in, and we are unaware. He comes in with his camouflage. He is a deceiver. The devil convinces man of his (Satan's) power, and by this means creates fears, phobias, confusion, and a feeling of helplessness.

This happens not because the devil cannot be overcome, but because man listens to his voice. We need to train ourselves to hear Jesus saying, *"All power is given unto me"* (Matt. 28:18).

There are times God does not see fit to heal, even when a child of God fulfills all of the conditions for exercising dominion. It is a mystery held within God's sovereign hands. Satan uses such things to tempt us to doubt God, but we know that God must have a higher plan.

Undoubtedly, God chooses to glorify Himself through the grace and peace He gives to His children—and sometimes this grace is made most impressive through a suffering saint. I have seen many of God's children walk through life in such an afflicted manner, and even in their weak condition they are not miserable victims. They have victorious faith. Theirs too is dominion.

Dominion over Devils

The Christian community must recognize that an aggressive war is being waged on all fronts by unseen and formidable foes. We must exercise dominion over the powers of the spirit world in order to reach the masses of this generation for Christ.

Many men and women of this world are more aware of the spirit realm than are many Christians. This very ignorance places the believer in a losing position in the battle with *"the rulers of the darkness of this world"* (Eph. 6:12). We must know our enemy in order to defeat him. We must also be familiar with the clear New Testament pattern of exercising authority over devils. The apostles set men and women free and wrought tremendous victories for the kingdom of God. It must be the same today. Whenever a possessed person comes in contact with a Spirit-filled disciple, there must be an instantaneous battle for deliverance. If not, the evil spirit will always openly mock the disciple.

When I am confronted with people whom I suspect may have an evil spirit, I ask them if they would accept Christ as their Savior. It doesn't matter what former experiences they have had; I ask them if they would accept Him then and there. And I ask them to say the sinner's prayer.

If they have a spirit in them, the thing often starts acting up immediately. It starts squealing, screaming, writhing, or something similar. After they have told me their story, I lay hands on them and command the spirit, whatever kind it is, to loose them and let them go free. And they are delivered.

In the Bible it never took a long time to set anyone free. When we start working with a person for a long time, we are not doing it the biblical way. If we pray for a person and he is not delivered, we had better back off by ourselves, talk to God personally, and then come back to them. Having a possessed person roll on the floor, screaming and yelling, is not what sets him free. Faith sets people free.

Instruments of Dominion

Without dynamic faith, born in the Christian heart at conversion and nourished through the Word of God, a believer cannot successfully battle against demon power and win. When a person is challenged by temptation or disease or the devil, his faith must constantly come into focus. He must have faith to command God's power. God explained that He desires we command Him. *"Thus saith the LORD, the Holy One of Israel, and his Maker, Ask me of things to come concerning my sons, and concerning the work of my hands command ye me"* (Isa. 45:11).

Abraham exemplified this ministry of commanding God. When he and the Lord were looking down upon Sodom and Gomorrah and God said He would destroy the cities, Abraham begged God for the salvation of the people there, saying if there were only fifty good people—or forty, or thirty, or twenty, or even ten—that God would not destroy them. Each time God was willing to meet Abraham's demand. (See Genesis 18:20–33.)

Man has never fully taken advantage of the true power of faith. God still waits for heroes of faith to use the divine dominion He gave Adam in the Garden of Eden. In the New Testament church, faith enabled Peter to tell the dead woman, Lydia, to rise up. By faith Paul cast out the powers of divination from the fortune-telling girl. Faith is the key that unlocks the generosity and strength of God. *"Without faith it is impossible to please him"* (Heb. 11:6).

Prayer is one of the most powerful instruments of the disciple. Prayer is actually the council chamber where divine commands are issued. In prayer the believer receives the solution to his problems. In prayer he receives the "infilling" of divine energy. Jesus revealed this when He prayed and fasted for forty days and then met Satan alone in the greatest spiritual struggle recorded in history.

Elijah demonstrated the power of prayer when he locked and bolted the heavens for three years with a single prayer. He further demonstrated this tremendous force when he called upon God to send rain upon the land. The apostle James specifically said Elijah was a common man as we are. (See James 5:17.) The difference is that *he* knew how to pray.

In the New Testament, Paul and Silas used this tremendous instrument of dominion when locked in the inner cell of the Philippian jail. At midnight they sang songs and prayed. The strength of their prayer shook the jail itself. It even resulted in the jailor's salvation.

All that prayer can accomplish has never been defined. It is still a great realm for research and exploration. But you must pray without ceasing if you wish to have dominion in prayer.

Still another instrument of dominion is action. God does not give power to the inactive. Jesus said, *"He that believeth on me, the works that I do shall he do also"* (John 14:12).

Dominion implies action. It is an act and not an idea. All through the Word of God we see that those who had dominion were men and women of action for God. God told Moses to have the people step into the water and He would do the rest. Jesus told a man with a withered hand, "Stretch it forth." He did the rest. (See Matthew 12:10–13.) In both instances, action was necessary before dominion was realized.

It is true that works alone are not sufficient for salvation. But some action is necessary, even vital.

Paul reminded the Corinthian Christians that there is work to do for the kingdom of God. *"For we are labourers together with God"* (1 Cor. 3:9). In James' epistle even stronger language is employed. *"What doth it profit...though a man say he hath faith, and have not works?...Faith, if it hath not works, is dead, being alone"* (James 2:14, 17).

It is not enough to know God's will. You must do it. One could know he had money in the bank and still go hungry and cold. He must go to the bank, withdraw some cash from his account, and spend it for food and warm clothing before his needs are met. Having it is not enough. Knowing about it is not enough. There must be action before it is of any value.

And so it is with Christian dominion. Before it pays off with bountiful blessings, dominion must be put in force with action on the part of the believer. In reality, dominion is an instrument to better enable the disciple to work for God and to obey His commandments. And His commandments have always been: "Go...do...give...work...."

By using the three instruments of dominion—faith, prayer, and action—we can be triumphant Christians. I urge you to stand up and have dominion with Christ, to be an overcomer and a blesser of mankind all the days of your life.

We can rejoice in the fact that the day is coming when the devil shall be bound (Rev. 20:1–3) and ultimately destroyed (Rev. 20:10). What a glorious hour it will be when there will be no devil and, because of that, no fear, no torment, no sin, and no sickness. Christian dominion over evil by the blood of Jesus Christ is not only meant for this life, but will carry into the world beyond the planet Earth. At this time Satan and his demons will have received their final reward in the lake of fire and will have eternally lost the earth to God and His saints.

We greatly rejoice when we read the last page of the Book. For you see, the saints win!

Notes

1. Augustine, *City of God,* Book 2, Chapter 25.

2. Roland Bainton, *Here I Stand* (Nashville: Abingdon, 1951), p. 362.

Appendix
Names for Satan and Demon
Spirits in the Bible

Names for Satan

1. Abaddon (Apollyon)

"And they had a king over them, which is the angel of the bottomless pit, whose name in the Hebrew tongue is Abaddon, but in the Greek tongue hath his name *Apollyon.*" (Rev. 9:11)

2. Accuser of the Brethren

"For the *accuser of our brethren* is cast down, which accused them before our God day and night." (Rev. 12:10) (See also Job 1:6–12; 2:1–7.)

3. Adversary

"Be sober, be vigilant; because your *adversary* the devil, as a roaring lion, walketh about, seeking whom he may devour." (1 Pet. 5:8)

4. Angel of Light

"And no marvel; for Satan himself is transformed into an *angel of light*." (2 Cor. 11:14)

5. Anointed Cherub

"Thou art the *anointed cherub* that covereth; and I have set thee so: thou wast upon the holy mountain of God; thou hast walked up and down in the midst of the stones of fire." (Ezek. 28:14)

6. Beelzebub

"But when the Pharisees heard it, they said, This fellow doth not cast out devils, but by *Beelzebub* the prince of the devils." (Matt. 12:24) (See also Matthew 10:25.)

7. Belial

"And what concord hath Christ with *Belial*? or what part hath he that believeth with an infidel?" (2 Cor. 6:15)

8. Corrupter of Minds

"But I fear, lest by any means, as the serpent beguiled Eve through his subtlety, so your *minds should be corrupted* from the simplicity that is in Christ." (2 Cor. 11:3)

9. Devil

"And the great dragon was cast out, that old serpent, called the *Devil,* and Satan, which deceiveth the whole world." (Rev. 12:9)

10. Dragon

"And there appeared another wonder in heaven; and behold a great red *dragon,* having seven heads and ten horns, and seven crowns upon his heads." (Rev. 12:3) (See also Revelation 20:2–7; Isaiah 14:29.)

11. Enemy

"The *enemy* that sowed them is the devil; the harvest is the end of the world." (Matt. 13:39)

12. God of this World

"In whom the *god of this world* hath blinded the minds of them which believe not, lest the light of the glorious gospel of Christ, who is the image of God, should shine unto them." (2 Cor. 4:4)

13. King

"And they had a *king* over them, which is the angel of the bottomless pit." (Rev. 9:11) (See also Ephesians 6:12.)

14. Liar

"Ye are of your father the devil, and the lusts of your father ye will do. He was a murderer from the beginning, and abode not in the truth, because there is no truth in him. When he speaketh a lie, he speaketh of his own: for he is a *liar*, and the father of it." (John 8:44)

15. Lucifer

"How art thou fallen from heaven, O *Lucifer*, son of the morning! how art thou cut down to the ground, which didst weaken the nations!" (Isa. 14:12)

16. Murderer

"He was a *murderer* from the beginning, and abode not in the truth." (John 8:44)

17. Oppressor

"How God anointed Jesus of Nazareth with the Holy Ghost and with power: who went about doing good, and healing all that were *oppressed of the devil.*" (Acts 10:38)

18. Prince of the Air

"...the *prince* of the power of the air." (Eph. 2:2)

19. Prince of Darkness

"...against the *rulers of the darkness* of this world." (Eph. 6:12)

20. Prince of this World

"Now is the judgment of this world: now shall the *prince of this world* be cast out." (John 12:31) (See also John 16:11.)

21. Roaring Lion

"Be sober...because your adversary the devil, as a *roaring lion,* walketh about, seeking whom he may devour." (1 Pet. 5:8)

22. Satan

"Now there was a day when the sons of God came to present themselves before the LORD, and *Satan* came also among them." (Job 1:6) (See also Revelation 12:9.)

23. Serpent

"But I fear, lest by any means, as the *serpent* beguiled Eve." (2 Cor. 11:3) (See also Genesis 3:1, 14; Revelation 12:9.)

24. Tempter

"And when the *tempter* came to him, he said, If thou be the Son of God." (Matt. 4:3)

25. Thief

"The *thief* cometh not, but for to steal, and to kill, and to destroy: I am come that they might have life, and that they might have it more abundantly." (John 10:10)

26. Wicked One

"When any one heareth the word of the kingdom, and understandeth it not, then cometh the *wicked one,* and catcheth away that which was sown in his heart." (Matt. 13:19)

Names for Demon Spirits

1. Spirit of infirmity (Luke 13:11)

2. Dumb and deaf spirit (Mark 9:25)

3. Unclean spirit, used 22 times (Matt. 12:43; Mark 1:23; Luke 9:42)

4. Blind spirit (Matt. 12:22)

5. Familiar spirit (Lev. 20:27; Isa. 8:19; 2 Kings 23:24)

Anglican evangelist Trevor Dearing says these "are evil spirits (not human) who are familiar with a dead person's appearance, habits, and life. They imitate the deceased in order to lead mourners astray—into occultism. Such experience is both real and supernatural. It also is false. It deceived my friend at St. Paul's, Hainault, who thought the medium was in touch with his wife and he became interested in the occult. Thousands have been tricked by this most cruel of the devil's deceits. Mediums, in their seances, are possessed by those familiar spirits. Familiar spirits have been known to visit bereaved people without invitation."

6. An angel (2 Cor. 11:14)

7. A lying spirit (1 Kings 22:22–23; 2 Chron. 18:21–22)

8. Seducing spirits (1 Tim. 4:1)

9. Foul spirit (Mark 9:25; Rev. 18:2)

10. Jealous spirit (Num. 5:14, 30)

My Challenge to You

If Jesus were to come today, would you be ready? If you are not sure, I invite you to receive Jesus as your Savior now. You will be filled with hope and peace that only Jesus can offer.

Pray this prayer out loud.

"Dear Lord Jesus, I am a sinner. I do believe that you died and rose from the dead to save me from my sins. I want to be with You in heaven forever. God, forgive me of all my sins that I have committed against You. I here and now open my heart to You and ask You to come into my heart and life and be my personal Savior. Amen."

When you pray the Sinner's Prayer and mean it, He will come into your heart instantly. You are now a child of God and you have been transferred from the devil's dominion to the kingdom of God.

Read 1 John 1:9 and Colossians 1:13.

—*Lester Sumrall*

About the Author

L ester Sumrall (1913–1996), world-renowned pastor and evangelist, entered full-time service for God after experiencing what he recalled as the most dramatic and significant thing that ever happened to him.

At the age of seventeen, as he lay on a death-bed suffering from tuberculosis, he received a vision: Suspended in midair to the right of his bed was a casket; on his left was a large open Bible. He heard these words: "Lester, which of these will you choose tonight?" He made his decision: He would preach the Gospel as long as he lived. When he awoke the next morning, he was completely healed.

Dr. Sumrall ministered in more than one hundred countries of the world, including Soviet Siberia, Russia, Tibet, and China.

He established Feed the Hungry in 1987. In addition, he wrote over 130 books. His evangelistic association (LeSEA), headquartered in South Bend, Indiana, is still actively spreading God's Word. Dr. Sumrall's goal was to win one million souls for the kingdom of God, and the ministry continues this vision. LeSEA ministry includes such outreaches as the World Harvest Bible College, radio and television stations, a teaching tape ministry, and numerous publications.